Varieties of English

Varieties of English

G. L. BROOK

Smith Professor of English Language and Medieval English Literature
University of Manchester

Macmillan

St. Martin's Press

First published 1973 by
THE MACMILLAN PRESS LTD
London and Basingstoke
Associated companies in New York Toronto
Dublin Melbourne Johannesburg and Madras

Library of Congress catalog no. 72–90233

SBN 333 14284 5

Printed in Great Britain by
RICHARD CLAY (THE CHAUCER PRESS) LTD
Bungay, Suffolk

Contents

Preface

THE aim of this book is to show how varied is the language that we use every day. The varieties examined fall into three categories, which can be associated with groups of speakers, with individuals, and with the occasion respectively. I have throughout been concerned with the English language as it is today and no previous knowledge of the history of the English language is assumed, but I hope that the book will be of use to students at colleges of education and universities and in the upper forms of schools as well as to the general reader. I hope too that those who are learning to use English as a second language will find here some help in the task that they have undertaken.

My thanks are due to the Librarian and Governors of the John Rylands Library, Manchester, for permission to use material from my article 'Varieties of English', published in the *Bulletin of the John Rylands Library*, LI (1968-9) pp. 271-91, and to the editors of *Leeds Studies in English* for permission to use material from my article 'The Future of English Dialect Studies' in volume II, n.s. (1968) pp. 15-22 of that journal. I am indebted too to my wife, who has read the proofs and advised me on many points, to Mrs Beryl Gaffin, who has typed successive drafts of the book with patience and skill, to Miss Sheila Ralphs for advice on Italian loan-words, and to my present and former students, especially Mr John Turner and Mrs Linda Berman, for keeping me informed about what they are doing to the English language today.

February 1972   G. L. B.

List of Abbreviations

A.E.	American English
B.E.	British English
C.O.D.	*The Concise Oxford Dictionary*
C.U.P.	Cambridge University Press
M.E.	Middle English
M.U.P.	Manchester University Press
O.E.	Old English
O.E.D.	*The Oxford English Dictionary*
O.F.	Old French
O.U.P.	Oxford University Press
S.P.E.	The Society for Pure English

Phonetic Symbols

THE letters p, b, t, d, k, g; f, v, s, z, h, w; l, r, m, n have their usual English values. The symbols given below are pronounced like the italicised letters in the key-words which follow.

CONSONANTS

tʃ	*ch*ur*ch*	ʃ	*sh*oe
dʒ	*g*em	ʒ	mea*s*ure
ŋ	si*ng*	ç	German i*ch*
θ	*th*ink	x	German a*ch*
ð	*th*en	j	*y*ou
ʍ	*wh*en	ʔ	The glottal stop, as in Cockney bu*tt*er

VOWELS

i:	s*ee*	ɔ:	s*aw*
i	s*i*t	u:	s*oo*n
e	s*e*t	u	p*u*t
æ	c*a*t	ʌ	b*u*tter
ɑ:	f*a*ther	ə	fath*er*
ɔ	h*o*t	ə:	b*ir*d

DIPHTHONGS AND TRIPHTHONGS

ei	d*ay*	ɔi	b*oy*
ou	g*o*	iə	h*ere*
ai	m*y*	ɛə	th*ere*
au	f*ou*nd	uə	p*oor*
ɔə	f*our*	aiə	f*ire*
		auə	p*ower*

Square brackets are used to enclose phonetic symbols.

A colon after a phonetic symbol indicates vowel-length.

A short vertical stroke above the line indicates that the following syllable is stressed, as in [tʃæs'taizmənt].

I

Introduction

FROM time to time popular books on English grammar are published with titles like *Is It Good English?*, and even more frequently newspapers publish letters from readers who express their loathing of this or that feature of pronunciation or syntax. From such publications one might gain the impression that there are only two varieties of English – the good and the bad – but this is a serious over-simplification. Many criticisms of linguistic habits arise from a failure to realise that there are many varieties of English and to recognise the characteristics of each variety. Thus, conversation is sometimes criticised because it does not conform to the rules of the written language, and British readers have condemned Americans because they choose to write in American rather than in British English. A very common cause of bad speaking or writing is the use of the wrong variety for a particular occasion: talking like a book, or using slang on a formal occasion, or failing to use slang on an informal occasion. Other critics recognise the existence of British and American English as varieties, each with its right to exist, but raise an outcry if there is any sign of borrowing from one variety into the other.

Attempts to resist such borrowing are pointless and doomed to failure. Just as English has borrowed words from many different languages, words and usages will continue to be borrowed from one variety of English into another. Such borrowing can be carried out clumsily with incongruous results, but that is not a good reason for trying to avoid it altogether. Another group of ill-founded criticisms results from a failure to recognise that a variety of English may have several subdivisions. Many letters to newspapers condemn as American importations linguistic constructions that are simply vulgarisms, which an educated American would avoid just as firmly as an educated Englishman would.

Part of the problem in learning a language is that, once learnt, it has to be used for so many different purposes, and each purpose calls for a different variety of the language. Max Beerbohm has illustrated the problem with his customary lucidity:

By its very looseness, by its way of evoking rather than defining, suggesting rather than saying, English is a magnificent vehicle for emotional poetry. But foreigners don't much want to say beautiful haunting things to us; they want to be told what limits there are, if any, to the power of the Lord Mayor; and our rambling endeavours to explain do but bemuse and annoy them. They find that the rewards of learning English are as slight as its difficulties are great, and they warn their fellows to this effect.[1]

It is natural that there should be varieties of language, since language is a form of human social behaviour, and communities tend to split up into groups, each displaying differences of behaviour. Language reflects these differences. The primary function of language is to convey ideas from one person to another, but these ideas may be information, command or entreaty. Language is used to make it clear whether we are well or ill disposed towards the person addressed, or it may simply be a way of calling attention to ourselves, the equivalent of a mild, deprecating cough, which may itself be a form of language. Language is used for a purpose similar to the tuning-in of a radio set. Two people may be so completely in accord that no tuning-in is necessary, but more often there are such differences of age or outlook that some adjustment is needed. The more completely two people are in sympathy with each other, the fewer words are necessary. Most people find that, however stimulating conversation with members of other age-groups may be, the society of their contemporaries is restful because a common background can be taken for granted without a lot of explanation.

Another reason for the existence of different varieties of any language is the variety of speakers of that language. Different

[1] Max Beerbohm, 'On Speaking French', in *And Even Now* (Heinemann, 1920) pp. 292–3.

speakers of English vary greatly in the extent of their vocabulary and in their skill in using it. They have to acquire this skill while using the language. Samuel Butler said that life was like playing a violin solo in public and learning the use of the instrument as you go along. It is no wonder that some of the early efforts should differ from those of a practised speaker or writer.

It cannot be too strongly emphasised that belief in the necessity for tolerating many different varieties of a language does not necessarily arise from indifference. It is only by allowing freedom of choice that we can encourage the development of language that is worthy of praise. The man who thanks God that all human beings do not look alike is not indifferent to the occasional beauty of the human face. One group of varieties of language has long been known and frequently studied: the varieties known as dialects. A dialect may be defined as a subdivision of a language that is used by a group of speakers who have some non-linguistic characteristic in common. The most common shared characteristic is a regional one: people who live in the same place tend to talk alike. But the link, instead of being regional, may be social or occupational. Sometimes a variety of language seems to depend not on the people using it but on the occasion when it is used. The same man will use widely different varieties of language in speaking on the telephone, in addressing a public meeting and in talking to his wife, and if he fails to make any distinction, his wife is likely to call attention to his failure. Such varieties have sometimes been called *situational dialects*, but the term *register* has recently come into use to describe varieties of this kind.[1] There are some varieties which can be regarded either as occupational dialects or registers. The distinction should perhaps depend on the extent to which their use becomes habitual. Liturgical language or the language of legal documents can best be regarded as examples of register, but if a parson asks you to pass the salt in musical bell-like tones that indicate his profession, he may be said to have acquired an occupational dialect. Professor Strevens[2] suggests a third category beside dialect and register

[1] See P. D. Strevens, 'Varieties of English', in *Papers in Language and Language Teaching* (O.U.P., 1965) pp. 74–86.

[2] Ibid., p. 84.

to describe the linguistic effects of the social relation between speaker and hearer. To these varieties of language he tentatively gives the name *style* or *manner of discourse*. Such varieties of language as respectful or patronising speech come under this heading. Social relationships undoubtedly have their effect on language, but it is not necessary to make a separate category of them; they can very well be included under register. On the other hand, it seems necessary to add to dialect and register a third category of varieties, which Professor Strevens does not mention: those to be associated with idiolects. These are linguistic characteristics shared by large numbers of people who seem to have no other characteristics in common. The word *question* is pronounced [kweʃtən] by speakers from many different places and belonging to many different social groups, and there is an even greater difficulty in assigning the various pronunciations of *gaseous* or *inveigle* to any regional or class dialects. Similarly, readiness to use slang, euphemism or swearwords is to some extent a question of register, but it is also a question of idiolect, a matter of personal preference. Dialect has been the subject of frequent comment, whereas register and idiolect have received little attention. All these varieties can be regarded as a series of overlapping circles, of which we all make use whenever we use the language.

Beside the three categories of dialect, idiolect and register, each of which comprises several subdivisions, there is one distinction that cuts across all of them: the medium of expression. There are at least three such media, namely speech, writing and gesture, but in English the third of these is comparatively unimportant. Gesture language, like picture language, resembles speech in consisting of a small natural element, smaller than is generally supposed, together with a much larger conventional element, which has to be learnt. Picture language is used in road signs, and every effort is made to reduce the arbitrary conventional element in these as much as possible so that they will be understood by foreigners or others who have not memorised their conventions. The meaning of some signs is immediately obvious, but some, like the torch formerly used to represent a school, are based on a poetic convention a knowledge of which cannot always be taken for granted, while others, like the exclamation mark, simply turn the knife in the wound of those who fail to understand them. Similarly, even such familiar gestures as nodding or shaking the head are conventional, not natural, gestures. The deaf-and-dumb alphabet is a highly conventional gesture language, based as it is upon two sets of conventions: the written alphabet and the gestures used to represent the letters. Other conventional gestures develop as jokes, such as that of pretending to turn a little handle, which remains in use to represent a cinema long after it has ceased to correspond with the realities of cinematic projection. Another widely understood sign is an imitation of the motions of milking a cow to ask someone to pass the milk. The further refinement of passing the hand in front of one's eyes, to show that the milk is pasteurised, is indulged in not from necessity but from delight in ingenuity. Such gestures are the slang of gesture language. The use of such gesture language is discouraged by teachers of the deaf, who prefer their pupils to master the art of lip-reading so that they can take part in general conversation.

Most varieties of language can be expressed in either speech or writing, but each variety is more at home in one or the other. Thus, in present-day English at least, regional dialects are most at home in the spoken language, although it is possible, by means of a number of compromises with spelling, to write poems and stories in dialect. On the other hand, the language of literary criticism belongs more properly to the written language. A good deal of criticism consists of attempts to attach exact meanings to such terms as *classical* and *romantic*. Legal language finds expression in both writing and speech, in the language of legal documents and the conventional formulas used in a court of law respectively.

The study of varieties of a language is rendered even more complicated by the existence of an extra dimension, that of time. In the past students of literature have sometimes assumed that the only important function of language was to preserve literature, and for them the study of the history of their language was obviously important. It is perhaps no accident that the greater attention which is paid today to the synchronic study of language has gone side by side with a greater awareness of the importance of the spoken language for non-literary purposes.

Sometimes as a joke a speaker will deliberately transfer into a new register the language that he has learnt in a different environment. An ex-serviceman who had deliberately refrained from expressing an opinion on his wife's new hat complained that he had been booked for dumb insolence. A customer in a bank, feeling that he was being neglected, was able to secure the speedy attention of a counter-clerk by calling out 'Shop!' in a loud, clear voice. The counter-clerk was resentful but the customer felt much better. The Duke of Edinburgh is said to have described the journey from Sandringham to Buckingham Palace as 'going back to live over the shop'. More often, the use of an inappropriate register is the result of a lack of linguistic tact and arouses contempt or embarrassment in the hearer. The American dramatist Moss Hart describes a conversation with a fellow-guest about his collaborator George Kaufman:

> 'What I really wanted to know,' she said, 'is aren't you frightened to *death* of him? You've written all those plays together and I don't see *how* you do it. Truly, Mr Hart, aren't you scared of George Kaufman? Just a little teentsy-weentsy bit? 'Fess up, now.'
>
> I suppose, at least I have thought since, that it was the phrase "Fess up, now' that made me behave very badly indeed, and I am not, as a rule, a rude person. I can, on occasion, summon up a passive resistance that will see me through even the dullest of dinners. But at the combination of 'teentsy-weentsy' and ''Fess up now', something snapped inside.
>
> Dream Girl either heard the snap – it seemed to me quite audible – or was aware of it physically, for she turned on the teeth again and said, 'Am I boring you, Mr Hart?'
>
> This time, I didn't hesitate. 'Frankly, yes,' I said. 'You are boring the living b'jesus out of me!'
>
> The smile froze on her lips.[1]

'Where does he come from?' is only one of the questions that can be answered when a stranger has spoken a few sentences and it is not the most interesting or important question. Others are 'To which social class does he belong?', 'Has he a high

[1] *Six Plays by Kaufman and Hart* (New York: Modern Library ed. 1942) pp. xviii–xix.

opinion of himself or of the people he is talking to?' and, most important of all, Elizabeth Bennet's question 'Can he be a sensible man?' Not all these questions can be answered with complete certainty on the basis of a few sentences, any more than a regional dialect can be identified with certainty on the basis of a similar amount of evidence, but it is remarkable how often it is possible to reach a provisional conclusion quite soon. Interviews on which a good deal depends are often conducted to answer such questions about a candidate rather than to test the profundity of his thought.

In all parts of the world today we can see and hear different languages and dialects competing with one another. It is often said that no one language is intrinsically better or worse than any other; it would be better to say that no reliable method has been found of measuring the relative merits of different languages. It is with languages as with human beings: some are better at one thing and some at others. One thing, however, seems clear: in the competition between different languages non-linguistic factors count for more than linguistic. The reason for the disproportionately wide spread of Indo-European languages in the world today has very little to do with the subtleties of the Indo-European verbal system, but it has a great deal to do with the historical fact that at certain significant points in the world's history people who happened to speak Indo-European languages were very successful conquerors, colonisers and traders. This is no doubt the reason for the extreme virulence with which questions of linguistic usage are discussed by people with few linguistic interests. Americanisms are feared and hated by Englishmen who think that we are in danger of losing our national identity, and the dialectal differences in British English that arouse most interest are those of social classes rather than those of regions, because competition between social classes has a great effect on the happiness and influence of individuals.

Varieties exist in all languages, and it is clear that learning a language is a more complicated matter than is sometimes supposed. It is worth asking whether the existence of a large number of varieties of a language is a nuisance to be resisted when it cannot be ignored, or whether these varieties serve any useful purpose. The matter is not one in which we have very much choice; one thing that is certain about language is that it is capable of putting up very strong resistance against the attempts of individuals to change it. But even if we had the power to reduce the number of varieties of English in existence, it is not at all certain that we should be wise to do so. It may be that we should be better off without dialects, but the world would be a much less interesting place if the idiolects that reflect human personality were all to go. Language is only one aspect of behaviour, but it is an important one, and if, by some miracle, we all began to talk alike, there would be some reason to fear that before long we should all behave alike in other ways. Registers, too, add to the interest of life. To choose only one instance, the varying degrees of intimacy that are possible in personal relations are all reflected in language, and it would be a pity if a lover and his lass were to talk to each other in a style suitable to a public meeting. It is inevitable that there should be many varieties of language and this is not a matter for regret, but we must face the fact that the existence of these varieties makes any language more difficult to use, both for natives and for foreigners. The difficulty has its compensations: difficulties make a language more interesting and more useful when the difficulties are mastered. Another consequence of the difficulty caused by the varieties of language is that greater tolerance is called for. In the hands of a master the wide range of English makes it a superb instrument for the expression of ideas and emotions, but in the hands of the rest of us this superb instrument is capable of playing many false notes, and we always have to be prepared for misunderstandings resulting from the faulty use of language or lack of sensitivity on the part of the hearer or the reader.

Each of the categories of spoken and written English has produced a group of varieties whose characteristics have arisen from the nature of the medium. For example, the limited capacity of the human lungs imposes a strain on a speaker who tries to utter long sentences without pausing for breath. Consequently, sentences in the spoken language tend to be shorter than in the written language, and even in the middle of a sentence a speaker will often pause to refill his lungs without realising that he is doing so. The pauses lessen his discomfort, but a good speaker gets into the way of using them to make his speaking more effective; frequent pauses lessen the strain on the hearer as well as on the speaker. Every sentence, except the very shortest, has a number of points, not always indicated in writing by punctuation marks, at which a slight pause will hardly be noticed or may be a positive advantage. For example, in the present sentence the gaps indicate points where slight pauses would hardly be noticed. A speaker may intend that a pause *should* be noticed, and he can achieve this result by prolonging the pause or by deliberately choosing to pause at a point where a pause would not naturally be expected. Young preachers often give an impression of earnestness by pauses of this kind. There are dangers in the practice. At a time when the British Government was being widely accused of lethargy, a speaker rose to its defence. After saying 'The Government is fully conscious —', he paused slightly and an interrupter seized the opportunity to say 'Oh no, it bloody well isn't.' The most important difference between spoken and written English is that the former can draw on a much wider range of methods of expression. Some important aspects of speech, such as stress and intonation, are capable of almost infinite variation in the spoken language, whereas in the written language they are hardly expressed at all. Obvious variations in stress and intonation can be expressed clumsily in the written language by means of punctuation: an exclamation mark indicates a sharp rise in pitch, a question mark a less violent rise and a full stop falling pitch. Italics can be used to show that a word is strongly stressed. Variations of tempo are used to express meaning in speech more frequently than we realise. Gestures and facial expression are also used in speech; a smile may be used to tone down an insult, and frowns and uncomprehending looks all play their part in the exchange of ideas. Before speaking to anybody we generally try to catch his eye to make sure that he is listening and, when this is impossible, many people are guilty of the practice, which causes much embarrassment to the blind, of speaking about a blind man in his presence as though he were incapable of speaking for himself: 'Does he take sugar in his tea?'

The invention of the tape-recording machine has made many people realise for the first time how much the spoken language relies on devices that are not available to the writer, but more than a century ago the novelist Bulwer Lytton printed what he claimed was a transcript of the words used by an upper-class Englishman in giving an account of an accident:

> 'No – I assure you – now err-err-that-er-it was the most shocking accident possible-er-poor Chester was riding in the Park-er-you know that grey-er-(substantive dropped, hand a little flourished instead) -of his-splendid creature! -er-well sir, and by Jove-er-the-er- (no substantive, flourish again) -took fright, and-e-er' – (here the gentleman throws up his chin and eyes, sinks back exhausted into his chair, and after a pause adds, 'Well, they took him into-the shop-there-you know-with mahogany sashes-just by the Park-er-and the-er-man there-set his what d'ye call it-er-collar bone; *but* he was-er-ter-ri-bly-terribly' – a full stop. The gentleman shakes his head, – and the sentence is suspended to eternity.
>
> *England and the English* (1833) pp. 89 f.

To most of Lytton's contemporaries this passage no doubt seemed an exaggerated parody, but it does not differ very much from the literal transcripts of tape-recordings of actual speech that can be taken down today. Such passages, when spoken, appear to be perfectly natural and intelligible, but a written transcript isolates a single constituent of a very complicated speech-situation. When the passage is spoken, the hearer relies on intonation, gestures, facial expression and significant pauses that are partially or completely ignored in the transcript. If a speaker takes warning from such a transcript and completes his sentences, he is likely to be accused of 'talking like a book'.

At the other extreme to the everyday speech recorded by Bulwer Lytton we have the carefully prepared piece of 'fine writing', which used to be much more popular than it is today. If the art of writing can be compared to a window of plain glass which allows the author's meaning to be clearly visible, such purple passages represent the art of the maker of a stained-glass window, who is anxious to create a thing of beauty in itself. A good example is the description of Leonardo da Vinci's 'La Gioconda' in Walter Pater's *The Renaissance* (1873):

The presence that rose thus so strangely beside the waters, is expressive of what in the ways of a thousand years men had come to desire. Hers is the head upon which all 'the ends of the world are come', and the eyelids are a little weary. It is a beauty wrought out from within upon the flesh, the deposit, little cell by cell, of strange thoughts and fantastic reveries and exquisite passions. Set it for a moment beside one of those white Greek goddesses or beautiful women of antiquity, and how would they be troubled by this beauty, into which the soul with all its maladies has passed! All the thoughts and experience of the world have etched and moulded there, in that which they have of power to refine and make expressive the outward form, the animalism of Greece, the lust of Rome, the mysticism of the middle age with its spiritual ambition and imaginative loves, the return of the Pagan world, the sins of the Borgias. She is older than the rocks among which she sits; like the vampire, she has been dead many times, and learned the secrets of the grave; and has been a diver in deep seas, and keeps their fallen day about her; and trafficked for strange webs with Eastern merchants: and, as Leda, was the mother of Helen of Troy, and, as Saint Anne, the mother of Mary; and all this has been to her but as the sound of lyres and flutes, and lives only in the delicacy with which it has moulded the changing lineaments, and tinged the eyelids and the hands. The fancy of a perpetual life, sweeping together ten thousand experiences, is an old one; and modern philosophy has conceived the idea of humanity as wrought upon by, and summing up in itself, all modes of thought and life. Certainly Lady Lisa might stand as the embodiment of the old fancy, the symbol of the modern idea.

The author of this passage is seeking to gain an effect by the piling-up of images in the manner of poetry, and his exact meaning is not easy to understand, although the separate words are for the most part familiar. In some varieties of English the author's meaning is obscure because he uses a large number of technical terms whose meanings are known only to specialists. Examples could be chosen from almost any scientific textbook. Here is an example from a manual of heraldry, a description of the coat of arms of the City and County Borough of Nottingham:

Gules, issuant from the base a ragged cross couped vert between two ducal coronets in chief or, and the lower limb of the cross enfiled with a like coronet. Crest: on a wreath of the colours, or and gules, a castle, walled, triple-towered and domed proper, the dome of the dexter tower surmounted by an increscent argent, and the sinister by an estoile or. Supporters: on either side, standing on a staff raguly erased, a royal stag guardant proper, ducally gorged or.[1]

In the comparison between spoken and written language, the advantages are not all on one side. Writing has obvious advantages not as a rule shared by speech: reader and writer do not have to be in the same place at the same time, whereas, until recently, speaker and hearer had to be; a reader can choose his own speed, re-reading the difficult passages and skimming lightly over the parts that seem to him unduly prolix. Most important of all, writing is more permanent than speech. For most of the purposes for which language is used, permanence would be a real drawback and we should all be much more taciturn if we thought that our trivial remarks were being recorded to be studied by others. Recent inventions have done something to lessen the disadvantages of the spoken, as compared with the written, language: radio has lessened the limitation of place and the record-player and tape-recording machine have lessened that of time. No doubt we are only at the beginning of an era of the preservation of recorded speech, but the student of literature will always depend heavily on the written word. On the other hand, the written language has a few devices that help to make one's meaning clearer. Some homophones are distinguished from each other by differences of spelling, like *kerb* and *curb*, *metal* and *mettle*, *flour* and *flower*, *sun* and *son*, but these do not amount to much, since the context usually makes it easy to tell which word is meant. Quotation marks are perhaps an exception to the rule that punctuation marks are less efficient than speech-variations. A skilful speaker can make it clear by his intonation that he is quoting, but some speakers have little confidence in their power to do this, with the result that we get clumsy devices like 'and I quote' or the

[1] F. E. Evans, *Discovering Civic Heraldry* (Shire Publications, Tring: 1968) p. 2.

reporter's 'quote' and 'unquote' to mark the beginning and the end of a quotation. One university teacher had a habit, which many of his students found endearing, of indicating a quotation by raising both hands to the level of his head and twiddling his fingers to represent the shape of quotation marks, but this was an individual eccentricity. A device that has become common among radio news-readers is to pause slightly before a word that would in the written language be enclosed within quotation marks. The device can become a way of expressing distaste for what one is reading; the reader uses the pause to disclaim responsibility for a word that he regards as badly chosen.

In early times the written language had little influence on the spoken language; with the spread of literacy the influence has become greater. Perhaps the most noticeable result of this influence has been the spread of spelling pronunciations like [weistkout] for [weskit]. The converse practice of spelling a word as it is pronounced, rather than as it was formerly pronounced, can have interesting results. Many people have been puzzled by the activities of a folk-heroine called Emma Chizzit before discovering that the name is a jocular spelling used to transcribe a frequent pronunciation, mainly but not exclusively Australian, of the question 'How much is it?' A less common result of the influence of the written language is the practice of spelling out some of the abbreviations commonly used in writing, such as *i.e.* and *e.g.* An advertisement stressed the importance of 'enclosing an sae'. A reader is likely to be puzzled by the use of *sae* without the full stops that are generally used to indicate abbreviations; the advertiser expects the reader to know that *sae* means 'stamped addressed envelope', and the use of the indefinite article with final -*n* shows that he expects him to pronounce it as three separate letters, not as a word.

The spoken and written varieties of English have tended to diverge. A hope expressed in the early days of broadcasting was that it might succeed in encouraging the use of a literary style more in accordance with speech. No doubt it has had that effect, but not to so great an extent as might have been expected. We all get into the way of accepting and understanding particular forms of speech or writing without even thinking of imitating them. A man whose everyday conversation was conducted in the measured tones of a B.B.C. announcer would soon be ridiculed out of the practice. The spoken word is acquiring greater prestige, and the practice of writing in a colloquial style is the deliberate aim of many writers, especially essayists.

One beneficial result of broadcasting is that it has introduced many people for the first time to good speaking and so has raised the standard of speech. Before the coming of broadcasting there was a tendency to treat spoken English, apart from the stage and the pulpit, as something suitable for everyday use but as less respectable than written English. Much is said of the tendency of broadcasting to discourage the use of dialect, but there is more variety in broadcast English than some of its critics suppose, and broadcasting has led many dialect speakers to be more tolerant of standard English. Another possible effect of broadcasting may be to discourage the disintegration of the English language, since it has brought spoken British English into parts of the English-speaking world which might otherwise have been dependent wholly on the printed word for their knowledge of English.

The vocabulary and sentence-structure of speech differ from those of the written language. The extent of the differences is soon realised by anyone who revises the notes of a spoken lecture for inclusion in a book. Individuals vary in their spoken style, but some lecturers, and those often the best, have to give up the attempt at translation entirely and, when asked for a written version of a successful spoken lecture, settle down to write a new essay on the same subject. A broadcast talk generally uses the syntax of the written rather than the spoken language; the hearer is conscious of the script although he cannot see it. The broadcast speaker has the task of anyone who is reading aloud: how to present the syntax of the written language through the medium of the spoken language for which it was never intended. Some idea of the rhythm of a passage presents itself even to the silent reader, but the man who is reading aloud has to decide for himself many problems of intonation and tempo.

Among the varieties of English there is one that in the opinion of many people is the only variety that matters. This is standard English. We have got into the way of speaking about standard English, but it does not follow that anyone speaks it. The term is a convenient abstraction, like the average man or the Identikit portrait of a wanted criminal. This statement will be disputed by many people who claim that they always speak standard English, but a careful listener will usually be able to notice many ways in which they diverge slightly from the norm.

Standard English is difficult to define, but the same difficulty applies to other aspects of behaviour, such as handwriting or dress. Corresponding to unintelligible speech we have illegible handwriting and slovenly dress. There are usually broad similarities between the dress of men living in the same country, but no two of them dress exactly alike. It is nevertheless possible to classify handwriting, dress and speech into broad groups having certain features in common. Within these groups variations will not be noticeable, except by the specialist. There are further parallels between speech and handwriting and dress, to mention only a selection of the innumerable aspects of human behaviour. They are all constantly changing under the influence of fashion. They are not homogeneous for any one person at all times. For example, any individual may speak or dress with varying degrees of formality according to the occasion. In most matters of behaviour most of us try to be sufficiently like other people to avoid being conspicuous, without trying to be exactly like anyone else. We try to share the characteristics that most of our fellow-men have in common. If we succeed in doing this with our speech, we shall be regarded as speakers of standard English, though a listener with a good ear for sounds might be able to detect in our speech many individual eccentricities.

2

Dialects

THE average upper-class Englishman of the older school is as reluctant to believe that he speaks a dialect as he is to believe that he can be a native. He assumes that natives come from Asia or Africa and that dialects are spoken by picturesque countrymen belonging to the lower income groups. The unfortunate pejorative associations of the word 'dialect' make it hard to give it a precise meaning that will be generally accepted. The question what is the difference between a dialect and a language does not admit of a clear-cut solution. Whatever criterion is applied, one finds instances where the conclusions that we reach on theoretical grounds conflict with those of common sense or with popular usage. A political test has been suggested: that a language is officially accepted as a national form of speech, whereas a dialect is not. This test breaks down by reason of what it excludes. For political reasons the language of a minority group may have no official recognition, but it would be absurd for this reason to treat as a dialect a form of speech belonging to a different family of languages. Welsh and Gaelic are languages, whatever recognition the British Government may give them. A literary test seems equally inadequate: to say that a language is a form of speech that has given rise to a literature, whereas a dialect has not. The test would err on the opposite side to the political test: it would cause us to regard as languages varieties of English such as the West Midland dialect of Middle English or the dialect of nineteenth-century Lancashire, which have produced a distinctive literature but which cannot properly be regarded as distinct languages. A better approach to the distinction is a purely linguistic one: if the speakers of one community can understand the speakers of another without a previous study of their way of speaking, then the two communities may be said to speak the same language. The drawback of this test is that 'understand' is not a word that can be defined with any precision; there are degrees of understanding. We have probably all attended lectures where we knew the meaning of each separate word used but where the words put together in sentences seemed to have no meaning at all. When this happens, no doubt some blame attaches to the speaker or the hearer or both, but it is only in the most figurative sense that they can be said to be using different languages. An adequate working definition of a dialect is that it is a subdivision of a language used by a group of people who have some non-linguistic characteristic in common. The difficulty of finding a definition that will distinguish between a dialect and a language reflects the facts of the situation: the distinction between the two is not precise, and therefore any precise definition would be an inaccurate one. Most languages probably began as dialects and, in course of time, the differences between two divergent dialects became so marked that it was more reasonable to regard them as separate languages. Dialects are not all alike in prestige, and criteria such as the possession of a literature or political recognition may cause one dialect to be more highly regarded than another. A Scottish or Irish accent is a less serious obstacle to social advancement than an English regional accent, and it may sometimes be a positive asset. No doubt the chief reason for this is that Scotland and Ireland are, or have been, separate countries.

There is a similar lack of precision when we try to decide what are the characteristics of any dialect. Every dialect is made up of a large number of idiolects and no dialect is completely homogeneous. All that we can do is to notice that in certain areas certain trends predominate. The area over which one dialect feature extends may not be identical with that given over to another feature that is thought to be characteristic of the same dialect, but if we superimpose upon one another maps recording the boundaries of various changes, we do find a certain approximate correspondence that enables us to speak of a dialect boundary. The boundary is not a line but a belt of land of variable width, where we may expect to find a mixture of forms from two dialects.

It seems clear that the relation between British and American English is that they are different dialects of the same language, but any expression of this opinion is likely to be misinterpreted

as a suggestion that only one of these varieties of English is a
dialect and is therefore in some way inferior to the other variety,
which one happens to speak oneself. The different varieties of
English in use overseas, as well as British English, are all regional dialects of the same language, which it is convenient to call
English, and each of them has many sub-dialects, both regional
and social. The view of dialect that should be resisted is that it
involves deviation from a norm. Standard English, which, as
its name implies, is regarded by many as a norm, is simply one
sub-dialect of British English which, for various historical
reasons, has come to enjoy special prestige in some circles while
in others it arouses dislike or amusement.

   Those who say that it will soon be too late to make a survey of
English dialects are taking too narrow a view of dialect. They
are chiefly interested in dialects that can be most easily traced
back to Old and Middle English, and they find these dialects
most readily among the older generation of country-dwellers.
There is nothing wrong with this preoccupation and there are
good practical reasons both to explain and to justify it. During
the nineteenth century and the first few decades of the present
century, scholarly interest in language was mainly historical,
and it was therefore sensible to pay attention to those dialects
that threw most light on the history of the English language.
There was a further argument: since language is constantly
changing, it is reasonable to begin by studying the dialects of
the older generation, for older speakers are likely to die sooner
than their juniors. There is a third reason why we have no
grounds for complaining of the choice made by the pioneers of
English dialect study: the dialects on which they concentrated
were those that were the easiest to study, and when we are
studying anything so complicated as human speech, there is a
lot to be said for starting with the simplest varieties that can be
recognised and using them as standards of comparison in the
study of more complicated varieties of speech. Dialect workers
do not as a rule use the word 'easy' in describing their task, but
when the pioneers of dialect study were confronted with a
complicated speech situation, they took the view that here was
something too complex to be profitably studied. The word most
often used to describe country dialects is 'pure', and the quality
indicated by this metaphor is consistency. A consistent dialect

is most likely to be used by speakers who have lived in the same village all their lives, avoiding contact with people with other speech-habits.

Professor Strevens makes a distinction between *dialect* and *accent* which I find hard to accept. He says:

> When two varieties of English (or of any other language) differ in patterns of grammar and vocabulary, they are different dialects; if their grammar and vocabulary are more or less identical but they differ in sound-patterns, then they are the same dialect but different *accents*.[1]

Such a definition excludes from the field of dialect all those differences in pronunciation which, because they are less easily borrowed than words, form the most valid basis of the division of a language into dialects. It seems better to take dialect to include differences of pronunciation and to avoid the use of the word 'accent' as far as possible, since the word has so many different meanings.

Everyone speaks both a regional and a class dialect. The two kinds of dialect are difficult to separate: there are regional variations in every class dialect and class variations in every regional dialect, but regional variations become less strongly marked as the speakers ascend the social scale. The greater mobility of educated people tends to lessen their regional variation. Lloyd James[2] distinguishes between a broad band of regional and class variants and a considerably narrower band of variants that have a great measure of similarity. The narrow band has more features in common with Southern than with Northern English. Those who speak any one variety of the narrow band are recognised as educated speakers throughout the country. There are varieties of English that are accepted over the whole of England and others that are not.

The question whether the use of dialect should be deliberately encouraged in present-day England is one on which more than one view is possible. The burden of making out a case rests on the users of dialect. The ordinary common-sense view would be that regional variations are a nuisance, liable to interfere

[1] Strevens, p. 80.
[2] In *Broadcast English*, S.P.E. Tract No. 32 (1929) p.9.

with efficient communication, which is the primary purpose of language. Lovers of dialect are moved by many different feelings, not all of them linguistic, and those who are hostile or indifferent find it hard to understand why dialects should arouse such strong feelings. The secret of their appeal usually lies in early associations. People who spent their childhood among dialect speakers try more or less unconsciously to recapture the glamour of their past years which seem happier in retrospect than they did at the time. Stories told in dialect have a strong appeal when they illustrate the way of life of the speakers of the dialect; nothing is to be gained by translating stories into dialect. Dialect literature is liable to seem particularly arid to readers who have no knowledge of the spoken dialect which it seeks to portray, because for them it cannot recapture the varieties of intonation and quality of voice that gave life to the spoken language. In much the same way later generations of readers find it hard to understand the enthusiasm which writers about the music-hall feel for some of the songs which they quote. Robbed of the music and the personality of the performer, the words of a music-hall song seem banal and trivial.

Regional novelists often make a successful use of dialect in their novels, and some of them are, or were in their youth, dialect speakers. Arnold Bennett's biographer says of him:

He took with him to London a high-pitched accent which rhymed 'class' with 'gas', a habit of pronouncing 'either' as 'eether', a tendency to drop his 'h's when his feelings were disturbed, and an oddly persistent inattention to the grammatical use of the personal pronoun: 'If other people can hit the popular taste, why not me?'[1]

The deliberate use of dialect, like that of slang, can tone down the severity of a rebuke. A speaker on the B.B.C. said that he found it impossible to resist the appeal of a notice placed near a pencil-sharpener in Broadcasting House: 'Please do not use this pencil sharpener for wax pencils or crayons. It mucks it up something awful.' A speaker may use dialect to cover up the embarrassment that he feels on being praised. A fairly common

[1] Reginald Pound, *Arnold Bennett* (Heinemann, 1952) p. 72.

North Country reply to praise for lavish hospitality is 'Aye, we're short o' nowt we 'ave'.

Differences in pronunciation among the English regional dialects are very numerous indeed. Two things need to be emphasised: boundaries between one pronunciation and another do not necessarily coincide with county boundaries, and the areas within which we can find one fairly homogeneous dialect are often much smaller than counties. To speak of '*the* Yorkshire dialect' or '*the* Lancashire dialect' is therefore an over-simplification. On the other hand the average man with few linguistic interests goes to the other extreme in his attitude to dialectal pronunciations and is content to notice a few features which he thinks of as Northern and a few which he regards as Southern, beside the distinctive varieties of English spoken in Scotland, Wales and Ireland, which he can recognise without analysing them very closely.

Perhaps the most obvious difference between Northern and Southern speech is in the pronunciation of what is usually spelt *a* before the voiceless fricatives [f], [s] and [θ] belonging to the same syllable. In the South the vowel is like the *a* in *father* [ɑː] but in the North it is like the *a* in *cat* [æ]. When the fricative consonant is followed by a vowel, the preceding vowel is not lengthened, even in the South, with the result that in standard English we find *classic* [klæsik] beside *class* [klɑːs] and *passage* [pæsidʒ] beside *pass* [pɑːs]. The variation is not affected by accidental differences of spelling, such as the doubling of the *s* in *class* and *pass*, or the use of *au* for the vowel and *gh* for the final consonant in *laugh*. A further difference between South and North is in the treatment of the short front vowel usually spelt *a* [æ], whatever the neighbouring sounds may be. In the South this vowel is often slightly raised while in the North it is often retracted. The result is that, to a Northerner, a Southerner often seems to be pronouncing *cat* as [ket] and confusing the difference between *man* and *men*.

Features of Southern dialects are less obvious than northern-isms, since standard English is based on the East Midland dialect of Middle English, which falls within the area that most people today think of as the South. There are, however, some dialectal pronunciations common in upper-class Southern speech which cannot be regarded as standard English. One of

these is the tendency to monophthongise the triphthongs
[aiə] and [auə] to [ɑː], as in [ɑː fɑː] *our fire*. A change that has
been taking place in Southern English during the last thirty
years or so is the tendency to raise and lengthen the vowel [ɔ]
before *l* followed by a consonant, as in words like *solve* and
resolve. Sometimes the *l* later disappears, and we then get
[souv] and [rizouv].

Dialectal pronunciations can give rise to homophones, which
may lead to confusion between a dialect word and a standard
English word. A traveller asking at an inn for a double room
was given a large glass of Jamaica rum. An Englishman who
told an American that he was a clerk was surprised to get the
offended reply, 'And I suppose you go "Tick tock".' To
American ears the [ɑː] of B.E. [klɑːk] resembles the vowel
which many Americans use in *clock*. A theological student,
describing his college course to a member of his congregation,
said that it included Doctrine. He was puzzled by the comment,
'So I suppose you are going to be a medical missionary.' The
inquirer had never heard of *doctrine* but she had heard of
doctoring: it was an important part of the training of a medical
missionary.

In the study of dialectal pronunciation we are not concerned
merely with the quality of vowels and consonants; stress and
intonation are also important and so too are differences of
vowel-length. Unfamiliar rhythms can interfere with intelli-
gibility. When Englishmen complain of the American drawl
and when Americans complain of British clipped syllables, they
are calling attention to differences of rhythm between British
and American English.

In syntax we find in dialects constructions that are exactly
parallel to those found in standard English. Students of the
history of English are familiar with the development of the
group genitive, which has enabled *the kinges sone of Engelond*
to become *the king of England's son*. A Lancashire girl achieved
an admirable example of a group genitive by describing a
woman as 'him as I go out with's mother'.

Many words have been borrowed from dialects into standard
English. *Brash* (pushful, cheeky) is now thought of as chiefly
American, but it is one of many provincial words reintroduced
into British English from America; the sense may have been

influenced by *rash*. *Elevenses* was originally dialectal; it is now a colloquial term for a mid-morning drink or snack. *Intake* was at one time chiefly found in Scotland and the North of England, where it meant 'enclosure'; a district of Sheffield has the name *Intake*. The noun is now in general use to describe persons or things admitted; it is commonly used in universities to describe students admitted to a university department each year. *Natter* is a useful North Country word, now coming to be used more generally. It means 'to keep on grumbling'. *Ploy* is a North Country word meaning 'undertaking, occupation', now used colloquially. The sense 'shrewd trick' was spread by Stephen Potter in *Gamesmanship*. *Pot-hole* (deep cylindrical hole worn in rock) is given as a northernism in the *English Dialect Dictionary*. The derivative *pot-holing* is used as a colloquialism in standard English to describe the exploration of caves. The word is useful for those who find *speleology* too pretentious and the American *spelunking* too informal. *Raffish* (disreputable, dissipated) and *tatty* (shabby) are adjectives that were originally dialectal but are now in general use.

There are many dialect words which have no exact equivalent in standard English, and which scholarly writers have, with varying degrees of success, tried to popularise. Logan Pearsall Smith would have liked to introduce into standard English such words as *thole, nesh, lew, mense, foison, fash and douce*.[1] Carlyle introduced *lilt* and *outcome* into literary English and Burns extended the life of *eerie, gloaming* and *croon*. The romantic movement introduced to literary use *glamour, gruesome, eldritch, uncanny, warlock* and *wraith* from dialects. A more recent borrowing is the preposition *agin* (against), used in a jocular way by people who do not normally speak in dialect, as in 'agin the Government'. American English has reinforced words which had become rare in British English but had never wholly died out. An example is *maybe*, which *O.E.D.* describes as 'archaic and dialectal'.

It is surprising to find that quite a large number of dialect words are of learned origin. Some of these, such as *tantum* (share), may have had their origin in students' slang. Others may have had their origin in technical terms which seem recondite to the general public but which are quite familiar to the

[1] 'A Few Practical Suggestions', in S.P.E. Tract No. 3 (1920) p. 9.

B

farmer. To this class may belong the botanical term *rhizome*, used in the expression *not a rhizome* (not a trace), found in the West Riding of Yorkshire.

Dialect speakers are fond of using vivid and imaginative phrases, often of their own coinage. One phrase that is used to describe an article of dress of which the speaker does not approve is 'I wouldn't be seen at a 'en-race with it'. Other disparaging phrases are 'like a dying duck in a thunder-storm' and 'He's like two-pennorth o' death warmed up'. A more precise insult is to call a self-righteous person an old white hen. This is an allusion to an anecdote about a woman who boasted about one of her hens: 'T'owd white hen never laid away but once and then t'egg were found'. The explanation may perhaps call for the further gloss that *to lay away* means to lay an egg in an unexpected place, thus causing extra work to the hen's owner. In some dialects the use of the pronoun *she* is resented. A protest against its use might take the form 'And who's she when she's at home?' A more idiomatic protest, frequently heard in the West Riding of Yorkshire, is ' "She" is t'cat's mother'. A housewife anxious not to appear too wealthy when she has just received her week's housekeeping money will say 'It's got its bonnet and shawl on', meaning that the money will not long remain in her purse.

The breaking down of the barriers between different academic subjects is one of the healthiest trends of the present time, and it is always very satisfying to find the explanation of a dialect word or phrase in some historical or geographical fact. A phrase meaning 'to keep on good terms with one's neighbours' is 'to keep t'band in t'nick'. *Band* means 'string' and *nick*, a variant of *niche*, here means 'groove' or 'hole'. The allusion is to an old-fashioned farmhouse door without a knob. There was a catch only on the inside, and the door could be opened from the outside by pulling a piece of string passing through a hole in the door. If the string, by accident or design, was not left passing through the hole, the door could be opened only from the inside. The phrase is a graphic way of describing a failure in communication of the kind represented by the countrywoman who said stiffly of her next-door neighbours: 'We don't speak to those people.' It is less easy to trace the origin of another useful North Country phrase: 'He tells you t'tale from t'thread to t'needle,' meaning that he spares you no trivial detail.

The rural communities where regional dialects still flourish are small enough to allow all the inhabitants of a village to know one another. Isolation from the outside world leads to the preservation of anecdotes about local celebrities. In such communities nicknames flourish, as they do for similar reasons in boarding-schools. A working man in one West Riding village was always known as 'Manager' and inquiries about the reason brought the reply that it was short for 'Aper, scraper, manager, japer', a masterpiece of concise character portrayal, indicating that the man in question was imitative, parsimonious, bossy and liable to indulge in practical jokes. Some phrases current in dialects incorporate proper names, which may sometimes be invented but which no doubt often preserve the names of local celebrities long since dead. Sometimes alliteration seems to have played a part in the choice or preservation of the name, as in *as throng as Throp's wife* (busy) and *as lazy as Ludlam's dog*, which was so lazy that it leaned up against a wall when it wanted to bark. The latter simile is widely current in Northern England, and the divorce between the phrase and any known person is illustrated by the large number of variants of the name Ludlam. Mr John Levitt[1] records from North Staffordshire alone the variants *Litheram, Letherum, Slitheram* and (by popular etymology) *Leatherman*. Mr Levitt records a number of other North Staffordshire phrases incorporating proper names. One of these has a special interest because the man referred to had more than local importance: *ready and willing as Spode's fiddle*. Josiah Spode (1733–1827) is best known as the inventor of English bone china, but he was also a violinist of some local reputation. Other Staffordshire phrases are *ready for Blind Charlie's cart* ('worn out', from the name of a Tunstall rag-and-bone man), *Kent's garden* ('Hanley cemetery', from the name of the first superintendent and registrar of deaths), *Corbett's bad luck* (a malingerer's complaint) and *Greggles's axe* (period of retrenchment in domestic spending after a holiday or some other spree).

Some of the phrases current in dialects are so widely used

[1] John H. Levitt, 'Some Aspects of North Staffordshire Vocabulary', *Journal of the Lancashire Dialect Society*, XIX (1970) 18.

that they can hardly be said to belong to regional dialect at all but rather to class dialect. There are many phrases descriptive of shrewdness. Victorian phrases such as 'Are you up to snuff?' and 'I'm awake' are no longer widely current, but there are other phrases such as 'He's got all his chairs at home', originating in a society so poor that the arrival of a few casual visitors made it necessary to borrow chairs from neighbours, who had to be vigilant to make sure that they were returned. Another phrase that reflects the poverty of the environment is 'He's had more sweethearts (or whatever it may be) than he's had hot dinners'. An expressive phrase to describe the feeling of being on top of the world is 'I wouldn't call t'king my uncle'.

Problems of communication caused by the use of dialect are not confined to unfamiliar words. A man who hears an unfamiliar word knows that there is a problem and either asks for an explanation or abandons the attempt at understanding. The words that cause most trouble are familiar words which have unfamiliar meanings in certain dialects. In 1967 the Ministry of Transport decided to change the wording on new level-crossing warning-boards because their use in Yorkshire was causing misunderstanding that might have had fatal results. The notices read 'Stop while lights are flashing'. To many Yorkshiremen *while* means 'until', and it was therefore found necessary to alter the word *while* to *when* (*Daily Telegraph*, 18 August 1967). Embarrassing moments can arise from the existence in British and American English of words and phrases which have improper associations in only one of those dialects. In England a man is said to be *on the make* if he is too much concerned with his own material success, but in America the phrase describes a man who is prowling around in pursuit of women. Americans are liable to gain an exaggerated idea of British hospitality when they hear an English girl invite new friends to knock her up some time. Other words that cause confusion include *knickers* (used in America in the sense of B.E. *plus-fours*), *pants* (used in A.E. as the equivalent of B.E. *trousers*; in B.E. *pants* often means 'underpants', though the American meaning is not uncommon in B.E.), *bill* (in A.E. it means 'bank-note'; in B.E. it is a demand for payment of a debt). The meaning of the sentence *It was a bomb* differs on the two sides of the Atlantic. In America the metaphor is regarded from the point of view of the man who drops the bomb and it therefore means 'a resounding success'; in England it is regarded from the point of view of the one on whom the bomb is dropped and it therefore means 'a complete disaster'. In British English the variant *bombshell* is more common. Some differences in usage arise from a difference of status of a given word in the two dialects. A plot of ground behind a house can be called a *backyard* on both sides of the Atlantic, but the word is more disparaging in Britain than in America. An Englishman may describe his garden as his backyard in humorous disparagement of his own possessions, but he will not expect his guests to do so.

The exact meaning of a word often depends upon the code of values prevailing in the community where it is used. It is difficult to convey the exact meaning of Irish *craytur* or Staffordshire *card*. Both words refer to someone whose conduct is open to blame, but both words imply more praise than blame. They express reluctant admiration for smartness or unconventionality.

With the decline of regional dialects, students of dialects will in future have to pay more attention to class dialects. Their study presents a number of problems, not least of which is the difficulty of defining a social class. The place where a man lives can be described in objective terms much more easily than the class to which he belongs, and the field-worker studying regional dialect is less likely than the student of class dialect to be asked by his informant what the blazes it has to do with him. One cannot completely avoid using terms like 'upper-class' and 'lower-class', but in general it is better to think of social classes in terms of areas rather than levels. One can, for example, regard as class dialects the varieties of English used by women, children or foreigners, all of which categories cut across a division into upper and lower classes. All groups are liable to develop words and phrases which serve, until they become generally known, to sort out strangers among them. It is said that people who work in *television* stress the first syllable of the word while the rest of us stress the third. Non-Catholics speak of the Pope while Catholics speak of the Holy Father. Such conventions quickly pass out of use when they are imitated by those who want to seem in the know. Public relations men

sometimes refer to Fleet Street with affectionate knowingness
as The Street, but we are assured that journalists who work
there never use the expression. It is not only exclusiveness that
leads to the preference for a particular expression. Some terms
are felt to be offensive by those whom they describe and are
avoided for that reason. A Scotsman is liable to be offended if
described as *Scotch* and will reply tartly that *Scotch* can be linked
with whisky or butter but never with a person, who should be
described as *Scottish* or *a Scot*. It is felt to be more courteous to
use the adjective *Jewish* than the noun *a Jew* and to speak of
a Chinese rather than *a Chinaman*.

The acquisition of the correct class dialect is an attainment
to which much importance has been attached in England,
especially by the middle classes. G. K. Chesterton tells how,
as a child, he was able to bring pressure to bear on his family:

> I screamed for a hat hanging on a peg, and at last in con-
> vulsions of fury uttered the awful words, 'If you don't give
> it to me, I'll say "at".' I felt sure that would lay all my
> relations prostrate for miles around.[1]

In the working classes the position is more complicated.
Two ambitions exist side by side: the desire to acquire the
speech-habits of a higher social class and the desire to show
solidarity with one's friends by rejecting as la-di-dah any
linguistic habits that they do not share. Sometimes, to the confusion of children, both ambitions exist in the same family,
husband and wife holding different views. The name of the
midday meal can cause trouble. In families where it is the chief
meal of the day it is generally called *dinner*; in families which
have dinner in the evening, the midday meal is called *lunch*,
and the use of this word is liable to cause resentment among
those who regard late dinner as the prerogative of a social
class to which they do not aspire. It is possible for the wheel
to come full circle. Barber[1] gives as an example of class dialect
the names for the course of a meal which follows the main
course: *pudding* (upper and middle classes), *sweet* (middle
class), *dessert* (lower middle class), *afters* (lower middle and

[1] *Autobiography* (Hutchinson, 1936) p. 15.
[1] Charles Barber, *Linguistic Change in Present-day English* (Edinburgh:
Oliver & Boyd, 1964) p. 17.

lower classes), after which the wheel comes full circle and we again find *pudding* (lower class).

Card games have their own vocabulary, and the choice of words is governed in part by class dialect. The scorn which Estella shows in *Great Expectations* for Pip, the boy who calls knaves *Jacks*, is well known, and most habitual players of card games could provide further examples. A bridge-player who referred to *dummy* was corrected by a stately lady opponent and required to say *table*.

In the choice of words and phrases class dialects are not rigid. The personality of the speaker has much to do with the choice of words, and all that one can say is that particular phrases are likely to be more frequent in a given social group than others. To express resentment on receiving a rebuke the normal lower-class male reaction would be a truculent intonation with a certain amount of swearing. Elementary irony of the type 'Pardon me for breathing, I'm sure' is perhaps to be associated with young women of the lower classes. The normal upper-class reaction from either sex would be rather pointed silence.

The study of class dialect is complicated by the existence of stereotypes. When variety artists want to make fun of the speech of any group of people, they choose a few easily recognisable characteristics, which become traditional. Members of those groups try to avoid the features which are frequently satirised, but there are many people who are more familiar with the satirical stereotypes than with the original, and music-hall imitations of speech are generally out-of-date. Sometimes people try to live up to stereotypes. No doubt many schoolboys have gone on saying that it was 'awfully decent' of someone to give them a tip because they felt that it was how adults expected schoolboys to speak.

Since upper-class English has more in common with standard English than has lower-class English, it is natural that its features should be less frequently the subject of discussion; there is more talk about what is 'non-U' than about what is 'U'. Many of those who indulge in the more extreme vagaries of upper-class speech are convinced that they are speaking standard English. There is no particular reason for associating this kind of English with one of the older universities rather than the other, but in popular speech it is described, especially by those who dislike it, as 'an Oxford accent'.

Lower-class speech at its best achieves a monosyllabic directness that has much to recommend it. The following is part of the evidence given in a court of law by a young man accused of assault:

> She said, 'You look like a ponce.' I said, 'Say that again and I'll clock you one.' And she said it again, so I clocked her one.

Much has been written in recent years about differences in vocabulary between upper-class and lower-class speech. Vocabulary is never a very reliable test of dialect, because of the ease with which words can be borrowed from one dialect into another, and frequent discussion makes such borrowing more frequent still. Certain turns of phrase can be associated, for a time at least, with particular social classes. The use of *civil* as a term of praise ('That's very civil of you') is a feature of upper-class dialect, while abbreviations like *chocs* (chocolates), *advert* (advertisement) and *comfy* (comfortable) belong to lower-class speech.

The semantic development of speech varies according to social classes. *Aggravated* in the sense 'annoyed' is easily defensible, but the use of the word in that sense must be regarded as a vulgarism, as must sentences like *It made me go queer all over*.

Popular speech shows a fondness for alliteration and rhyme, found in phrases like *It neither means nor matters*, and *I'll love you and leave you*. Rhyme is found in such remarks as *See you later, alligator*, and *In a while, crocodile*, which once had a passing vogue among young people, and in the more widely used comment on a difficult situation *Hell's bells*. A child in an air-raid shelter during the Second World War no doubt derived a certain melancholy relief from her sufferings when she reported 'Mum, my bum's numb'.

Love of rhyme or alliteration may lead to the use of a word that cannot be justified on the grounds of sense alone, as when we say that there is *neither rhyme nor reason* in something. Why should there be rhyme? Most people know what we mean if we complain of having to *toil and moil*, but the verb *moil* (O.F.

moillier) is obsolete in English except in this phrase, and the word owes its preservation to the appeal of the rhyming tag. We have grown accustomed to talking about the *brain drain*, and the rhyme has no doubt added to the popularity of the phrase, so that we tend to forget how discourteous the metaphor really is. During the Second World War, one North Country fish-and-chip shop was able to reconcile its customers to a reduction in the size of helpings by displaying a notice:

> *It's owing to Hitler*
> *That fishes are littler.*

One variety of substandard English is the genteel style which results from an attempt to avoid being vulgar. Muriel Spark has a short story 'You Should Have Seen the Mess'[1], which represents the language of a seventeen-year-old typist, prudish, class-conscious and censorious. Her admission that, although she was always good at English, she was not so good at other subjects, is followed by two exclamation marks. She complains that the stairs are 'far from clean' and 'far from hygienic'. She is shocked by the question 'Do you watch Telly?': 'I did take this as an insult because we call it T.V., and his remark made me out to be uneducated.' She makes 'nice friends' and meets people 'of an educated type' but their home does not satisfy her. 'There were contemporary pictures on the walls, but the furniture was not contemporary but old-fashioned, with covers which were past standing up to another wash, I should say.' She is the sort of girl who can be relied upon never to say 'It's me', but the use of 'I' for 'me' is different, and she says 'Dad would not dream of saying such a thing to Trevor or I'. This is the sort of language that is likely to result from an attempt to shake off substandard speech and to achieve refinement.

A group with shared interests is likely to develop a kind of linguistic shorthand in referring to those interests. The motive for the development of such allusions is partly a desire for secrecy and partly a desire for brevity, a single word being enough to remind the members of the group of a whole series

[1] In *The Go-Away Bird and Other Stories* (Macmillan, 1958; Penguin Books, 1969).

of events in the past. The use of allusions that are meaningless
outside the group increases its solidarity, and there are sometimes real advantages in secrecy, as in the well-known *F.H.B.*
('Family hold back') when supplies are running out, and the
less well-known reassurance *M.I.K.* ('More in kitchen').
Family varieties of a language are liable to cause exasperation
to the uninitiated, especially to those who marry into a family
that has developed its own linguistic habits. A. A. Milne
paints a convincing picture of this exasperation:

> 'Your family, like every other family, has a language of its
> own, consisting of unintelligible catch phrases, favourite,
> but not generally known, quotations, obscure allusions, and
> well-tried, but not intrinsically humorous family jokes. For
> instance, there was a constant reference last Christmas to
> somebody or something called Bufty.'
> 'Pufty.'
> 'I accept the correction without admitting that it is in
> itself elucidatory.
> 'It was terribly funny. It was when Raymond was four
> years old. . . .'[1]

One group of English class dialects consists of the varieties of
English spoken by those whose mother tongue is a language
other than English. Some foreigners, of course, learn to speak
English so well that the only mark of their foreign origin is
that they speak English more clearly and accurately than the
average Englishman, but some of them keep traces of their
original language in the difficulty that they have in pronouncing particular sounds, such as those represented by *th* in *then*
and *thin*, in their slightly unidiomatic choice of words, or in
their intonation. Lloyd James has pointed out how misleading
foreign intonation can be when superimposed on English:

> Much of our hasty generalization concerning the French
> temperament is due to the fact that French speakers use, in
> normal circumstances, types of intonation that are in
> English associated with situations that are not normal.
> Normal German intonations sound preposterously formal

---

[1] A. A. Milne, 'Christmas Party', in *A Table Near the Band and Other
Stories* (Methuen, 1950) p. 76.

when applied to our language by Germans speaking English. The simple and unobtrusive 'Thank you' used by the Britisher, uttered on a falling intonation, creates an impression of rudeness upon many Americans, who are accustomed to use for the expression of their gratitude an intonation that to many Britishers seems fantastically fulsome. And as a rule it is the intonation that hurts; English spoken on Swedish intonation may sound petulant, on Russian intonation lugubrious, on German intonation offensive, on French intonation argumentative, on many American intonations casual or cocksure, on Danish intonation flat and sombre.[1]

There are pitfalls for foreigners in polysemy, which allows one word to have several meanings. A German professor at an English university found himself embarrassed by frequent invitations to go for a walk with his colleagues. He tried to avoid further invitations by explaining that he took plenty of exercise: 'I walk to and from the University every day, so, you see, I have two motions a day.' On this occasion the foreigner felt no embarrassment, since he did not know that one of the meanings of *motion* is 'evacuation of the bowels', but an Indian visitor to England suffered needless embarrassment after learning the meaning of *toilet-roll*. He asked for some soap at a chemist's shop, and when asked if he wanted toilet soap, he blushed and replied that he only wanted to wash his face.

A translator with an imperfect knowledge of one of the languages with which he is concerned needs to be resourceful. A Frenchwoman in an English restaurant asked the waiter if *duckling* meant '*poulet*'. The waiter made his meaning perfectly clear by flapping his arms up and down and saying 'Poulet quack quack.'

A translator has the difficult task of deciding whether to produce a literal translation that will preserve the stylistic features of the original or to render its spirit within a quite different set of conventions. The problem is illustrated, with some exaggeration, in the first chapter of Kinglake's *Eōthen*:

I think I should mislead you if I were to attempt to give the substance of any particular conversation with Orientals. A traveller may write and say that 'the Pasha of So-and-So was

[1] A. Lloyd James, *The Broadcast Word* (Kegan Paul, 1935) p. 8.

particularly interested in the vast progress which has been made in the application of steam, and appeared to understand the structure of our machinery – that he remarked upon the gigantic results of our manufacturing industry – showed that he possessed considerable knowledge of our Indian affairs, and of the constitution of the Company, and expressed a lively admiration of the many sterling qualities for which the people of England are distinguished'. But the heap of commonplaces thus quietly attributed to the Pasha will have been founded perhaps on some such talking as this:

Pasha. The Englishman is welcome; most blessed among hours is this, the hour of his coming.

Dragoman (to the Traveller). The Pasha pays you his compliments.

Traveller. Give him my best compliments in return and say I'm delighted to have the honour of seeing him.

Dragoman (to the Pasha). His Lordship, this Englishman, Lord of London, Scorner of Ireland, Suppressor of France, has quitted his governments, and left his enemies to breathe for a moment, and has crossed the broad waters in strict disguise, with a small but eternally faithful retinue of followers, in order that he might look upon the bright countenance of the Pasha among Pashas – the Pasha of the everlasting Pashalik of Karagholookoldour.

Traveller (to his Dragoman). What on earth have you been saying about London? The Pasha will be taking me for a mere cockney. Have not I told you always to say, that I am from a branch of the family of Mudcombe Park, and that I am to be a magistrate for the county of Bedfordshire, only I've not qualified, and that I should have been a Deputy-Lieutenant, if it had not been for the extraordinary conduct of Lord Mountpromise, and that I was a candidate for Boughton-Soldborough at the last election, and that I should have won easy if my committee had not been bribed. I wish to heaven that if you do say anything about me, you'd tell the simple truth.

Dragoman – [is silent].

Pasha. What says the friendly Lord of London? is there aught that I can grant him within the Pashalik of Karagholookoldour?

Dragoman (growing sulky and literal). This friendly Englishman – this branch of Mudcombe – this head purveyor of Boughton-Soldborough – this possible policeman of

Bedfordshire is recounting his achievements and the number of his titles.

Pasha. The end of his honours is more distant than the ends of the earth, and the catalogue of his glorious deeds is brighter than the firmament of heaven!

Dragoman (to the Traveller). The Pasha congratulates your Excellency.

The author is writing a comic passage, not a literal record, but he has provided a good illustration of two different varieties of English.

Sometimes a new variety of English is provided by incompetent translation from a foreign language. Such translations often have considerable linguistic interest, since they throw light both on the original language and on that into which they are translated. Harley Granville–Barker discovered an English translation of Ibsen's *The Doll's House* that leaves the reader in no doubt that he is reading a translation.[1] The following is a specimen:

Helmer. . . . Has my thoughtless bird again dissipated money?

Nora. But Thorvald, we must enjoy ourselves a little. It is the first Christmas we need not to spare.

Helmer. Know that we cannot dissipate.

Nora. Yes, Thorvald; we may now dissipate a little, may we not? . . .

Helmer. Nora! (goes up to her and catches her in jest by her ear) Is thoughtlessness again there? Suppose that I borrowed £50 today, and you dissipated this sum during the Christmas week, and a tile fell down on my head New Year's eve, and I were killed—

Nora. O fy! don't speak so badly.

Helmer. Yes, suppose that such happened, what then?

Nora. If such bad were to happen, it might be indifferent to me either I had debt or no. . . .

Later in the play Nora says how charming it is to have 'excessively much money', but her husband explains to her that a forger cannot have a happy home life because 'a such atmo-

[1] Harley Granville-Barker, 'The Coming of Ibsen', in *The Eighteen-Eighties*, ed. Walter de la Mare (C.U.P., 1930) pp. 159–96.

sphere, containing lie, causes contagion and disease-substance in a home'. In the famous scene between Nora and her husband at the end of the play Nora expresses her hope that 'the most wonderful must happen' and yields to her husband's entreaty to say what this would be:

Nora. That cohabitation between you and me might become a matrimony. Good-bye.

Two large groups which might be expected to have some linguistic characteristics in common are the two sexes, but the groups are so large that it is doubtful whether any general statement of much value can be made about their speech-habits. Linguistic characteristics are closely linked with features of personality, and generalisations are usually prompted by hostility. It is not uncommon to find the same characteristic claimed by both men and women as characteristic of the opposite sex. Those who maintain that only prejudice can assign particular linguistic characteristics to one sex or the other will no doubt regard these characteristics as features of idiolect.

Part of the problem of associating certain phrases with either men or women is that those who are fond of a particular phrase are usually quite unaware how frequently they use it or how they differ from other people in their fondness for it. To a woman a particular word or phrase may seem to be characteristically masculine but to a man it is liable to seem the sort of phrase that anyone would use. How else could one say it? The use of the word *Honestly!* as an exclamation without any indication of what it is that the speaker honestly wishes to say, is perhaps a feminine characteristic. Another may be the ironical use of *Thank you very much* to show that the speaker is affronted. Women are more fond than men of using emphatic adverbs on trivial occasions: 'How tremendously interesting!', 'He was a terrifically gentle person', 'He is desperately anxious to'.

There are different conventions in swearing for the two sexes, in both frequency and choice of oaths, though here, as always, allowance must be made for individual variations. *C.O.D.* describes *drat* as 'a woman's imprecation' and Mr P. G. Wodehouse makes a further distinction:

Lady Bostock made a clicking noise, like a wet finger touching hot iron, which women use as a substitute for the masculine 'Well, I'll be damned!'[1]

It was for long a convention that for a woman knowledge of French or Italian was an elegant accomplishment, but that to be a good Latinist was rather frumpish. Old-fashioned public speakers have been known to say, with a patronising leer, 'I will translate that for the benefit of the ladies.' Such remarks are not often heard nowadays, perhaps because speakers realise that the members of his audience who will be in a position to correct his errors of translation are at least as likely to be women as men.

A desire to avoid giving offence can lead to the development of a style not far removed from duplicity, and women are sometimes said to have developed this indirect approach with greater subtlety than men. Arnold Bennett gives an example of this kind of talk:

'Did you, dear?' Mrs Hamps exclaimed, with great surprise, almost with shocked surprise. 'I'm sure it's beautiful. I was quite looking forward to tasting it; quite! I know what your gooseberry jam is.'

'Would you like to try it now?' Maggie suggested. 'But we've warned you.'

'Oh, I don't want to trouble you *now*. We're all so cosy here. Any time —'

'No trouble, Auntie,' said Clara, with her most captivating and innocent smile.

'Well, if you talk about "warning" me, of course I must insist on having some,' said Auntie Clara.

Clara jumped up, passed behind Mrs Hamps, making a contemptuous face at those curls as she did so, and ran gracefully down to the kitchen.

'Here,' she said crossly to Mrs Nixon. 'A pot of that gooseberry, please. A small one will do. She knows it's short of sugar, and so she's determined to try it, just out of spite; and nothing will stop her.'

Clara returned smiling to the tea-table, and Maggie neatly unsealed the jam; and Auntie Clara, with a face beaming with pleasurable anticipation, helped herself circumspectly to a spoonful.

[1] *Uncle Dynamite* (Herbert Jenkins, 1948) chap. 3.

'Beautiful!' she murmured.

'Don't you think it's a bit tart?' Maggie asked.

'Oh no!' protestingly.

'*Don't* you?' asked Clara, with an air of delighted deferential astonishment.

'Oh *no*!' Mrs Hamps repeated. 'It's beautiful!' She did not smack her lips over it, because she would have considered it unladylike to smack her lips, but by less offensive gestures she sought to convey her unbounded pleasure in the jam. 'How much sugar did you put in?' she enquired after a while. 'Half and half?'

'Yes,' said Maggie.

'They do say gooseberries were a tiny bit sour this year, owing to the weather,' said Mrs Hamps reflectively.

Clara kicked Edwin under the table, as it were viciously, but her delightful innocent smile, directed vaguely upon Mrs Hamps, did not relax. Such duplicity passed Edwin's comprehension; it seemed to him purposeless. Yet he could not quite deny that there might be a certain sting, a certain insinuation, in his auntie's last remark.

Clayhanger (1910) bk I, chap. 7

The student of the language of married couples has to concern himself with the linguistic implications of silence. One provoked wife declared that lack of small talk ranks with adultery as a cause of broken marriages, and more than one puzzled husband has been driven to ask 'Is it something I've said?' in an attempt to discover why the house has suddenly become rather quiet.

It is natural that parents should be keenly alert to the signs that their children are developing normally, and it is not surprising that a baby's first utterances should be the subject of absorbed interest. One very distinctive variety of English is that which some adults see fit to use in talking to babies. Much of this supposed baby-talk is imposed on babies by well-meaning adults. The sounds are produced by adults and received by babies in uncomprehending or embarrassed silence or else with little gurgles of delight that have their origin in a realisation that the speaker means well. The more extreme examples of baby-talk are too embarrassing to quote in

cold blood, but James Joyce provides an example of the sort
of imagery used in talking to very young children, who must
find that it greatly increases the difficulty, though it may add
to the interest, of the language that they are trying to learn:

> Edy straightened up baby Boardman to get ready to go and
> Cissy tucked in the ball and the spades and buckets and it
> was high time too because the sandman was on his way for
> Master Boardman junior and Cissy told him too that Billy
> Winks was coming and that baby was to go deedaw and
> baby looked just too ducky.[1]

Even when the baby produces the sounds, it is an adult who
attaches meaning to them, and a baby, trying out a few easy
groups of sounds like *mama* and *dada* is liable to be congratulated on the success with which he has recognised his parents.

Some conventional terms of reproach to children are used
so often that many of those who use them forget their real
meaning, with incongruous results. A cartoon in *Punch* showed
a girl holding a weeping baby sister and saying sternly, 'Don't
be a baby'. Extravagant children are sometimes told that
money does not grow on trees. This is reasonable enough, but
one mother was heard to reply to a child's request for a second
peach by the remonstrance: 'Peaches don't grow on trees,
you know'. Sometimes it is the child who uses the words without understanding their full meaning. A schoolgirl's essay on
climbing Mount Everest began: ' "Wake up, Jean", said my
sister one morning, "Father says that we can climb Mount
Everest today."' Speaking easily to children comes naturally
to some people but, if it does not, it is not an easy art to acquire,
since children are quick to resent any attempt to talk down to
them. Many parsons find the preparation of a sermon much
easier than that of a children's address, and the practice of
converting a sermon into a children's address by inserting
the words 'Boys and girls' at intervals is not an ideal one. A
similar practice is adopted by some unskilful authors of instructive books for children, who convert masses of miscel-
laneous information into unconvincing dialogue by the insertion at intervals of phrases like 'said John' and 'replied his
father'. There is a lot to be said for talking to children as

[1] *Ulysses* (Hamburg: Odyssey Press, 1932) i 378 f.

though they were adults. They will not understand everything that is said, but that is the normal lot of children in an adult world, and they will appreciate the compliment of a refusal to talk down to them. On the other hand a mother waiting for a bus was probably going too far when she said to the baby in her arms: 'Have we just missed a 62 then? Never mind, there'll be an 80 along in a minute.'

Those who have to look after young children often get into the way of using conventional phrases as good-humoured re-proofs. The disadvantage of their frequent use is that the child has time to think of a reply to be stored up in readiness for the next time that the cliché is used. One child replied to the re-proof 'Fingers were made before knives and forks' by saying 'Yes, but mine weren't', and another, when told 'You'll have to eat a peck of dirt before you die', replied 'Yes, but not all at once'. Some adults adopt a coyly indirect style when reprov-ing young children, goading them to mutinous fury by remarks like 'I know a little boy who hasn't washed his hands before tea', and 'Somebody's got out of the wrong side of the bed this morning'. Mrs Gaskell has recorded the resentment that such coy phrases can cause even to a good-tempered child:

> 'Oh! a little bird told us,' said Miss Browning. Molly knew that little bird from her childhood, and had always hated it, and longed to wring its neck. Why could not people speak out and say that they did not mean to give up the name of their informant? But it was a very favourite form of fiction with the Miss Brownings, and to Miss Phoebe it was the very acme of wit.
>
> *Wives and Daughters*, chap. 40

The language of children has been studied very thoroughly by Iona and Peter Opie, who have also studied nursery rhymes.[1] It is clear from their investigations that in the language of children there is both class and regional dialect. The con-versational small change of children consists largely of insults. It is rich in synonyms for 'Go away'. *Absquatulate, clear off, get lost* and *get stuffed* belong to the slang of earlier generations,

---

[1] Iona and Peter Opie, *The Lore and Language of Schoolchildren* (O.U.P., 1959). Most of the examples quoted here are from this book.

but their place has been taken by many other expressions. To these traditional insults there are equally traditional replies, and the art of casual conversation among children, as among adults, consists largely in remembering the right stock responses. An adult who replies to the greeting 'How do you do?' by saying that he is all right apart from a slight cold is not obeying the rules of the game. A child, on first going to school, has to learn what is the locally approved insulting reply to an insulting question designed to find out whether the newcomer is socially acceptable. The use of the word 'Well' is likely to provoke the question 'What's the use of a well without water?' In one school the correct reply to this is 'A monument with thee stuck in t'middle'. No other reply will be accepted. Some of these traditional replies are equivalent to a refusal to reply. They are the child's way of expressing resentment at an impertinent question. A frequent reply to the question 'Where are you going?' is 'There and back to see how far it is'. Another is 'Daft. Are you coming?' A reply to the question 'What time is it?' is 'Time you learnt more sense'. Some of these pert replies are at least as old as the eighteenth century and are quoted in Swift's *Polite Conversations* (1738). In reply to the question 'How old are you?' Swift's Miss Notable, like many a child of today, replies 'Why, I'm as old as my Tongue, and a little older than my Teeth', and in reply to the question 'Why do you sigh?' she replies 'To make a Fool ask, and you are the first'. Replies to an insult do not have to be subtle: 'And you're another' will meet most contingencies. Those who prefer figurative language may say 'Same to you with knobs on'.

Some ingenuity is shown in persuading other children to make remarks which can be construed as self-incriminatory. A famous question is 'If frozen water is iced water, what is frozen ink?' The child who falls into the trap will find himself called 'Stinker' for the rest of his school life.

Some phrases are not often used by children but owe their vogue to books written for children. Examples are *Honest Injun* and *Honour bright*. Other phrases are *God's honour*, *Straight* and *Criss-cross*. Another group of phrases is used to make it clear that there must be no going back on a bargain once it is made. Such phrases include *No backs*, *No back backers*, *No swops back* and *Chip, chop, can't have it back*. In private schools a child

who wants to give something away will say *Quis?* and the child
who first cries *Ego* receives the gift. Now that Latin is under
fire, we may expect these words to give way to the alternatives
Who wants? and *Bags I.* These terms are self-explanatory, but
there are many dialectal equivalents of *Bags I.* They include
ballow, bollars, chaps, chucks, cogs, sags and *jigs it.*[1] These words
are also used to claim a privilege, such as the first turn in a
game, but there are other words, especially in the North of
England, used only to claim first turn. The most common of
these is *foggy*, with variants *fuggy* and *feggy*. Other words are
ferry and *firsy*. When the first place has been claimed, competition is concentrated on the second place, for which the most
frequent words are *seggy* and *seccy*. If you want the last place,
you say *laggy* or *leggy*. These words can be used in the negative.
In reply to the question 'Which of you is going to help with the
washing-up?' there may well be replies *Bags not* or *Baggy no me.*
A shorter reply, which is itself negative, is *fains*, which is
roughly equivalent to *bags not*. It is probably the same word
as *fen*, used by Jo in *Bleak House* (1853, chap. 16) when he says
Fen larks, which he glosses *Stow hooking it.*

Many words are used by children who wish to gain a respite
in a game. This is usually accompanied by the gesture of
crossing the fingers. The words differ widely in different parts
of the country. They include *kings, cree, cruce, skinch, fains,
vains, fainites, barrels, bees, peas, parleys* and *creams.*[2] One of the
most widespread, as well as one of the oldest of these truce-
terms, is *barley*, which occurs in the fourteenth-century poem
Sir Gawain and the Green Knight (v. 296). The present-day use
of the word by children helps to explain the sense in which the
word is used in the poem. The wide variety of completely
different words suggests that it may be the crossing of the
fingers that indicates the real demand for a respite and that the
word that accompanies the gesture is comparatively unimportant.

Names are liable to malformation in a number of well-
established ways. Disyllabic Christian names are likely to be
shortened, especially by university students, so that we get
Dave, Pete and *Sue.* Monosyllabic surnames are likely to be

[1] Opie, p. 135.
[2] Ibid., pp. 141–53.

lengthened by the addition of *-y* to give *Smithy*, *Browny* and *Jonesy*. Forenames may be first shortened and then replaced by a rhyming name: *Richard* becomes *Rick* and then *Dick*, *Robert* becomes *Bob*, *William* becomes *Bill*, *Michael* becomes *Spike*. This practice is many centuries old and is not confined to children; it is the origin of a number of English surnames, such as *Hicks* and *Dixon*. The two processes of curtailment and lengthening may be applied to the same word: *Elizabeth* becomes *Bess* and then *Bessie*; *Robert* becomes *Bob* and then *Bobby*. Certain nicknames are traditionally attached to particular surnames, so that we get *Hookey Walker*, *Dusty Miller*, *Spud Murphy* and *Nobby Clark*.

Nicknames are used in great profusion. These may be such obviously descriptive names as *Ginger* or they may be puns on the surname, such as *Timber* for *Wood*. One rather erudite pun provided a nickname for a student of short stature, who was known as *Bildad* because Bildad was only a Shuhite. (Job ii, 11).

Many terms of abuse describe unpopular children: *clot*, *dumb cluck*, *erk*, *gawp*, *pig*, *rat* and *stinker*. Children respect natural ability but despise those who work hard. Such a one is a *swot* or a *swotpot*. The most common childish taunt is to say that another child is mentally deficient and there are many synonyms, such as *bats*, *batty*, *barmy*, *crackers*, *duffy*, *dippy*, *dotty*, *goofy*, *daft*, *potty*, *cuckoo* and *loco*. There are also phrases like *he has a screw loose* or *he is off his chump*. *Yob* (back slang for *boy*) has come to be used in a derogatory sense 'lout'.

Certain words are taboo. Opie says: 'Amongst boys to use the word "crying" is sometimes held to be almost as sissy as the act itself.'[1] The word 'weeping' is rather literary and is little used, but there are many synonyms, some of them dialectal, including *blubbing*, *blabbing*, *blabbering* and *slobbering*. Dialectal words include *booing* (South of England), *shriking* (Lancashire and Yorkshire), and *greeting* and *girning* (Scotland).

Public schools develop their own language in both vocabulary and idiom, which is sometimes more recent in its origins than its speakers believe. One of the aims of this special vocabulary is to keep outsiders outside, or, less unkindly, to foster a corporate spirit among the boys who attend the school. In one school play a housemaster is stiff from 'refereeing the sevens on bogger five'

[1] Opie, p. 186.

and he promises a boy 'a chimney to keep your nose clean about second tosher.'[1] Some words are used mainly by boys, and the use of such words in speaking to a master will be followed by an apology; others are used mainly by masters and some are used by both. To the first class belong *beak* (schoolmaster – not merely the Head), *impot* (imposition), *palaver* (a talk), *stoke* or *stoking* (work), *stush* (good), *sap* (shrewd); to the second class belong *the H.M.* (the Headmaster), *Sam* (the Senior Assistant Master), *leg* (promotion to a higher form) and *leg-moot* (meeting at which such promotions are discussed). Some are in general use at many schools; others are peculiar to one school.

In some schools 'Sir' is not merely a form of address; it becomes a common noun meaning 'schoolmaster'. The boys of one school were heard singing an ironical and possibly impromptu verse:

> Sir is wise and Sir is gentle;
> Sir is strong and Sir is mental.

In the language of children, as in adult speech, new words may be created almost by accident and then imitated because they satisfy a need. Sometimes the obscurity of the word is the source of its appeal. People enjoy the mystification caused by the use of a new word whose meaning is not at once apparent. The schoolboy who said that they did *gazintas* at school as part of their work in arithmetic created a word which was eagerly seized on by others, who were ready to explain to those who admitted defeat that two gazinta four but four does not go into two.

[1] *Daily Telegraph;* 25 May 1970, a review of a television play by Carey Harrison.

3

Idiolects

IDIOLECTS are among the most neglected subjects of linguistic study, but the material for their investigation lies around us on every side. Our own linguistic peculiarities do not form a good starting-point; our habitual use of particular pronunciations or idioms prevents us from realising how unusual they are. When we are listening to a good lecture, we are too preoccupied with the speaker's subject-matter to pay much attention to his manner of speaking, but a bad lecture provides ideal conditions for the study of the speaker's idiolect. The use of the term does not mean that each linguistic feature is unique, though no doubt each speaker is unique in the possession of a particular set of linguistic features.

A good example of a feature of idiolect is one that has taken its name from an individual who was addicted to it: the spoonerism, which consists of the transposition of the initial consonants of two adjacent words. The resultant groups of sounds may be nonsense, or one or both of them may be words different from those intended by the speaker. If the transposition is too neat, one suspects that the spoonerism has been constructed deliberately and artificially, as with *tons of soil* for *sons of toil*, but probably most people have come across examples that seemed genuine enough. One speaker said that she had often wondered what a *beaver's weam* looked like, and an excited examiner said that a candidate was no better than a *beery queta*, a phrase which appealed to his colleagues much more than the *query beta* which he intended.

There are phrases which tell us a good deal about the character of the speaker. Such phrases are: 'If I've told him once, I've told him a hundred times', 'No one has ever succeeded in convincing me', 'He got no change out of me', and 'Whether you like it or whether you don't like it'. The habitual use of such phrases reveals the nagger, the man wise in his own conceit, the braggart and the bully, but these are not social groups and such phrases must be considered matters of idiolect.

Variant pronunciations which cannot be associated with any regional or social group and which do not depend upon the occasion when they are used are all matters of idiolect. Historical causes of the variation can usually be discovered, but the choice of one pronunciation or the other is a matter of individual preference.

The most common cause of variant pronunciations is that a sound-change has taken place, sometimes several centuries ago, which has not been accepted by all speakers of English. It is sometimes possible to detect a dialectal distribution of a sound-change, but there remain a number of changes, examples of which are given below, where the distribution is largely a question of idiolect, though sometimes regional or class dialect has to be taken into account as well:

(1) Today a long open *o* [ɔː] in words like *loss, off* and *cloth* is old-fashioned, whereas most young speakers use a short vowel. Lengthening of *o* before [f] and [θ] took place during the eighteenth century in the speech of some people, and since then long and short vowels have existed side by side. With some speakers at certain times the long vowel is fashionable; with others the short vowel.

(2) There is a similar fluctuation between long and short *o* before *l* in words like *salt* and *falter*.

(3) There is some fluctuation between [juː] and [uː] as the development of M.E. [iu]. The [juː] has become [uː] after [tʃ], [dʒ] or [r]. After most other consonants [juː] has remained, as in *music, huge*, but after certain consonants, especially [s], [z] and [l], we find both forms, as in *suit, resume, resolution, illuminate*. In such words forms with [uː] are gaining ground, and in American English they are more common than in British English. In the nineteenth century [uː] seems to have been regarded as a vulgarism, and spellings suggesting the pronunciation are common in the dialogue of low-life characters in Dickens.

(4) The long vowels [iː] and [uː] are tending to become narrow diphthongs. The first element of each of the new diphthongs is slightly more open and more central than the second. The diphthongisation is most common when

the vowel in question occurs at the end of a word; it is frequently found, for example, in *shoe* and *sea*.

(5) Pre-tonic [e] generally becomes [i] in such words as *eleven* and *electric*. Many people say [e] in the first syllable of *electricity*, perhaps as a spelling pronunciation or because the syllable has secondary stress.

(6) There is alternation between [i] and [ə] in the lightly stressed syllables of many words. The [ə] is generally preferred in the North.

(7) The English language is notorious for its tolerance of heavy consonant groups, which may be even heavier than they seem at first because a single letter, like *x*, can represent two consonants. Some speakers are less tolerant of these heavy groups than they think, because they unconsciously simplify them by omitting one or more consonants in pronunciation. The word *texts* is not often pronounced [teksts]; sometimes the first [s] disappears, sometimes it is the final [ts]. In a radio discussion on education the word *sixth-formers* was used several times by all the speakers, but none of them pronounced it [siksθ-fɔːməz]. The favourite pronunciation was [siksfɔːməz] with variants [sikfɔːməz] and [sikθ-fɔːməz]. Assimilation of consonants to make pronunciation easier is common. Most people would be willing to agree that they voice the *s* in *dogs* but not in *cats*, but many of those who suppress the first *s* in *horse-shoe* would indignantly deny the charge. Similarly some speakers, but not all, pronounce the *t* in *postman, not bad* and *half past four*, while others suppress the *k* in *asked*. Many speakers pronounce only a single *p* in *lamp-post* and a single *m* in *Prime Minister*.

(8) Initial *h* generally disappears in lightly stressed words, such as *him* and *his*, especially when they are near to other words beginning with *h*.

(9) Final *r* is generally silent before a pause or a word beginning with a consonant. When followed by a word beginning with a vowel, the *r* is often pronounced, as in *here and there* [hiər ən ðɛə] beside *here they are* [hiə ðei ɑː]; this *r* is known as *linking r*. On the analogy of linking *r*, an *r* is often inserted in pronunciation without etymological justification between a word ending in a vowel and one beginning with a vowel, as in *India and China* [indiər ən tʃainə] or *the idea of it* [ði aidiər əv it]; this *r*

is known as intrusive *r*. After [ə] intrusive *r* is now very widely used, especially in the South. After other vowels, as in *law and order* [lɔːr ənd ɔːdə], it is nothing like so frequent but is probably becoming more common. In the attempt to avoid intrusive *r*, some speakers insert a glottal stop [ʔ], a sound that is common in substandard English (as in the Cockney pronunciation of *butter*).

Another reason for the rise of variant pronunciations is that there are various spelling conventions existing in English side by side. For example, the spelling *ei* represents [ei] in *eight* and [iː] in *receive*. When a speaker has to pronounce an unfamiliar word like *inveigle*, it is a matter of chance or individual preference which convention he follows. There are many words like *gaseous* and *hegemony* that we see in print several times before we have to pronounce them, so that we have to decide on the pronunciation for ourselves. Spelling pronunciations have been further encouraged by the spread of education; there are few spelling pronunciations in a language which to most of its users is merely a spoken language. Spelling pronunciations affect a number of everyday words, such as [fɔəhed] beside [fərid] 'forehead', [weistkout] beside [weskit] 'waistcoat', [ɔftən] beside [ɔfn] 'often', [klouðz] beside [klouz] 'clothes'.

Another cause of variant pronunciation is variation in the position of the stress in words of more than one syllable. For example, *alabaster* is sometimes stressed on the first syllable, sometimes on the third. Some disyllabic words, such as *protest*, *convict* and *increase*, have the stress on the first syllable when they are used as nouns but on the second syllable when they are used as verbs. Inevitably analogy sometimes takes place, with the result that we find *protest* and *increase* used as nouns with the stress on the second syllable. In polysyllabic words the stress tends to occur as near to the beginning as possible, but some speakers dislike the piling-up of lightly stressed syllables and heavy consonant groups which results and therefore they resist the tendency. Another influence that resists the tendency to throw the stress back is the analogy of words containing the same stem with different suffixes: *dispute* v. with stress on the second syllable leads us to put the stress on the third rather than the second syllable of *indisputable*, and the influence of *chastise* leads to [tʃæsˈtaizmənt] beside [ˈtʃæstizmənt]. The influence of the noun *presence* causes us to put the stress on the third syllable of *omnipresence*. Similar analogies do not as a rule affect *omnipotent* and *omniscience*, but they are always liable to do so with individual speakers, thus producing variant pronunciations.

Reduction of stress generally brings with it changes in the quality of vowels, which, when lightly stressed, tend to approach the central vowel [ə] or the front vowel[i]. It is quite easy to give to a lightly stressed vowel the quality that it would normally have in a stressed position, and here we have another source of variant pronunciations. Failure to centralise a lightly stressed vowel may be dialectal: in the North *condemn* is often pronounced [kɔn'dem] whereas in the South it is [kən'dem], and *Ascot* tends to be pronounced ['æskət] in the South but ['æskɔt] in the North. The treatment of lightly stressed vowels may sometimes be a matter of occupational dialect, since clergymen, accustomed to speaking slowly and carefully from the pulpit, are particularly liable to resist the tendency to reduce the quality of vowels. More often, however, it is a matter of idiolect. New conditions lead to changes in pronunciation. The first *e* in words like *sixpence* is usually reduced to [ə] or it may disappear altogether, leaving the *n* vocalic. Since the introduction of decimal currency into Great Britain some speakers have made a distinction, using the reduced vowel when they refer to old pence and a full [e] when they refer to the new decimal coins.

There is much variation between short vowels and long vowels or the diphthongs that have developed from them. Should the first vowels in *progress* or *evolution* be long or short? Most people pronounce *thesis* as [θiːsis] and *hostile* as [hɔstail] but some speakers pronounce these words [θesis] and [houstail]. *Patent* is pronounced [peitənt] by large numbers of the general public but [pætənt] by lawyers. Sometimes two different pronunciations of the same word have acquired different meanings for some, but not all, of those who use them. *Greasy* is pronounced with both [s] and [z]; some people take [griːzi] to mean 'slippery', literally and metaphorically, while they take [griːsi] to mean 'covered with grease'.

Variant pronunciations arise from differences in the treatment of foreign loan-words in English. The older practice was to treat a loan word like a native word as quickly as possible, substituting the nearest English equivalent for any sounds that did not occur in English. More recently we have tried to preserve the foreign pronunciation of loan-words. Words that have been assimilated may have signs of foreign origin, such as accents, restored and are often printed in italics: *rôle*, *détour*, *dépôt*. There are three stages:

(1) The loan word keeps its foreign pronunciation, as in *garage*.
(2) Sound-substitution is used to replace unfamiliar sounds, as in the pronunciation of *envelope* as [ɔnvəloup].
(3) The loan-word is anglicised, as in *carriage*.

The less familiar the language from which a word is borrowed, the more likely we are to resort to sound-substitution or to complete anglicisation, but there are many fluctuations caused by fashion, and individual words sometimes resist general tendencies. *Naïveté*, besides *naïvety*, shows the restoration or preservation of a foreign suffix, and *nuance* often resists the tendency to anglicisation. Even those who know Spanish are liable to seem affected if they use the Spanish pronunciation of *Don Quixote* in an English context. French is the foreign language best known to Englishmen, and there is therefore a tendency to pronounce any foreign loan-word as though it were French; some Englishmen pronounce *robot* (cf. Czech *robotit*, 'to work') as [roubou]. In native words and in early loans from French *ch* is pronounced [tʃ], as in *choose* and *chair*, but in many words derived from Latin or Greek it is pronounced [k], as in *machination*. Since the words of classical origin include many that are read more often than they are pronounced, their pronunciation is often influenced by the more familiar native words. The B.B.C. committee which made recommendations on the pronunciation of doubtful words[1] recommended that *ch* should be pronounced as [k] in *distich*, *hemistich*, *lichen* and *machination*, but pronunciations of all these words with [tʃ] or [ʃ] are occasionally heard. The same B.B.C. committee recommended that the Latin *pace* 'with deference to' should rhyme with *racy*. Unassimilated loan-words from Latin form

[1] Published in *Broadcast English*, reprinted as part of S.P.E. Tract No. 32 (1929).

a group of variant pronunciations of their own, since some speakers give them the 'old' pronunciation, which treated Latin words as though they were English, while others give them their 'reformed' pronunciation.

The pronunciation of a word may be modified to avoid confusing it with another word. It is in accordance with the tendencies that control English pronunciation that *laboratory* should have the chief stress on the first syllable, but fear of seeming to say *lavatory* causes many speakers to prefer the variant pronunciation with stress on the second syllable. Fear of confusion with *gorilla* causes some speakers to pronounce the *u* in *guerrilla*.

There are many varieties of speech which result from the attempts of individual speakers to steer between two extremes, both of which may be considered undesirable. There is a slip-shod speech in which consonants are under-articulated, and on the other hand it is possible to over-articulate them, and sometimes on-glides and off-glides are introduced to make sure that the consonants are clearly pronounced. Vowels may be drawled and, when this happens, diphthongisation is likely to take place; on the other hand they may be clipped short, as in one variety of military speech, giving an impression of smartness. We find similar variations in intonation, some people speaking monotonously, with little change of pitch, while others vary the pitch of their voices so much that they seem to be continually excited.

Another variety of speech that is not confined to a particular social group is the affected or mincing. Affectation in speech is the result of a deliberate attempt to acquire pronunciations that do not come naturally to the speaker, who has not a sufficiently good ear for sounds to make his imitations acceptable. It is not an easy characteristic to recognise with certainty, because subjective considerations often determine the use of the word. An impression of affectation may be given by unfamiliarity: Northerners sometimes claim that a long *a* in *path* is affected, but it is the normal Southern English pronunciation. When applied to speech, the word 'affectation' can be used to describe a striving after improvement that is either too conscious and deliberate or one that is unsuccessful. It is the sort of thing that a critic had in mind in saying that a colleague had 'a beautiful voice in the worst sense of the word'. Affectation can change the quality of vowels. In parts of the North of England the *u* of *run* [ʌ] is pronounced like the *u* of *put* [u]. A speaker trying to avoid the provincial [u] may go too far and produce a vowel like the *a* in *ran* [æ]. If he does so, he may reasonably be accused of affectation. In affected speech, vowels are liable to be too close, and the same thing can happen with the first element of a diphthong, so that we get *refained* for *refined*. Affectation is not a recent development in English. Chaucer says of the Friar:

> *Somwhat he lipsed, for his wantownesse,*
> *To make his English swete upon his tonge.*[1]

The differences between one idiolect and another are so marked that we can usually recognise anybody that we know at all well by their speech alone, but the most obvious differences are not variations in the quality of vowels and consonants but differences in the quality of the voice, in stress, intonation, tempo and facial expression. Confusion is liable to arise when speaker and hearer have different speech-habits. The most common reason for stressing an auxiliary verb is to reply to some contradiction or scepticism expressed or expected, but some speakers stress unimportant words for quite different reasons. A man unaccustomed to speaking in public, when called upon to make a speech, may stress words without realising that he is doing so. One speaker had the mannerism of stressing the word 'will', and he therefore announced 'There *will* be refreshments', with a stress that suggested that somebody had said that there wouldn't. Other speakers have the habit of stressing prepositions without implying the contrast that most people would intend if they stressed such normally unimportant words. Most husbands and wives know that to understand a speaker's meaning it is necessary to pay attention to much more than the actual words used, and the sensible ones learn to act on the information that they acquire from intonation or slight pauses without demanding that the speaker's real meaning should be spelt out in words. Bertie

---

[1] *General Prologue to the Canterbury Tales*, vv. 264 f.

Wooster shows an unexpected skill in phonetic analysis when reproving Jeeves:

> 'Jeeves,' I said, 'Don't keep saying "Indeed, sir?" No doubt nothing is further from your mind than to convey such a suggestion, but you have a way of stressing the "in" and then coming down with a thud on the "deed" which makes it virtually tantamount to "Oh, yeah?" Correct this, Jeeves.'[1]

We sometimes find howlers such as *ignorami* and *Mussulmen*, as the result of mistaken identification of a foreign ending. What is the plural of *mongoose*? Another common mistake is to use a foreign plural as though it were a singular; *data*, *memoranda*, *phenomena*, are all occasionally used in this way. Sometimes a distinction in meaning develops, as in *indexes* beside *indices*.

There are people who declare proudly that they speak only when they have something to say. They clearly think that such a policy is both logical and praiseworthy, but they are the cause of a lot of unnecessary suffering, because their silence is liable to be misunderstood by those who have a different attitude towards language. Most people like to exchange a few words with their acquaintances when they meet them, not with a view to conveying or eliciting information, but simply to show that they are well disposed towards them. This practice has become so widespread that silence on such an occasion is often interpreted as a sign of hostility. Even when it is recognised that silence has no hostile cause, failure to exchange greetings is generally resented and the word 'hazing' is used to describe the offence. The exchange of remarks purely from the motive of friendliness is known as phatic communion. Convention plays a large part in the choice of greetings. When relations between the two people concerned are rather formal, *Good morning* (or *afternoon* or *evening*) is usual; less formal is *Hello*, and young people often prefer *Cheerio* or *Hiya*. A brief comment on the weather sometimes serves as an alternative to these greetings. Here too there are degrees of formality. *Turned out nice* is rather staid; *Is it warm (cold) enough for you?*

---

[1] P. G. Woodhouse, *Right Ho, Jeeves* (Herbert Jenkins, 1934) chap. 9.

is familiar. In regional dialects one often hears *It's a warm (cowd) 'un*, to which the answer is *It is an' all* or *It is that*. It is a mistake to allow oneself to proceed to a comment on what the weather was like first thing this morning. These words bear a very different meaning according to the time of the day when the speaker or hearer began work.

After the weather, inquiries about health are the most frequent conversational counters. These inquiries must not be taken too seriously. One of the many definitions of a bore is that he is a man who, when asked how he is, tells you. Fairly common replies are *Not so bad* and *Just middling*; the important thing is to avoid detail. The conventional nature of the inquiry is most obvious at a formal introduction, when the normal response to the inquiry *How do you do?* is to repeat the question.

In communities such as colleges, where people are constantly meeting one another, phatic communion may fall into disuse, though its place may be taken by a slight relaxation of the rigidity of the face. Academic people, whose thoughts are often far away, have the reputation of being indifferent to the social obligations of conversation and some of them deliberately cultivate a reputation for taciturnity. On social occasions they are content to follow the example of Mr Rochester ('"Humph!" said Mr Rochester, and took his tea in silence': *Jane Eyre* chap. 13). One unfortunate young lady, sitting next to an eminent scholar at dinner, got only two remarks out of him during the whole meal: 'Is that so?' and 'Is that so also?'

It may seem unjust that men grow impatient with people who suffer in silence. The impatience is justified because the silence is rarely complete. There is usually a sigh or an injured expression to call attention to the suffering and the heroism with which it is borne. The silent suffering becomes an accusation. The comment of Ulysses on Cressida is an apt description of the way in which meaning can be expressed without the use of words:

> *There's language in her eye, her cheek, her lip,*
> *Nay, her foot speaks.*[1]

Thoughts can be expressed without words, and, conversely, words can be used without any real expression of thought.

[1] Shakespeare, *Troilus and Cressida*, IV. v. 55 f.

Mrs Gaskell describes a superficial woman's love of cliché when she says of Mrs Gibson in *Wives and Daughters* that 'her words were always like ready-made clothes, and never fitted individual thoughts' (chap. 28). Clichés are used as part of the small change of conversation without close examination of their meaning. There are many remarks which, if interpreted literally, are trite, but which are full of meaning if we take the trouble, as most of us do, to work out the speaker's real meaning. For example, 'I'm not so young as I used to be' means 'I am beginning to suffer from the disabilities of age'. During the Second World War the following exchange of consolatory remarks took place between two women:

'Well, never mind. Every day brings us one day nearer to the end of the war.'
'Ee, I wish I could think so.'

Clichés often defy grammatical analysis. Such a cliché is *as of now*, which may be due to imitation of commercial English. Others are used to gain time for the speaker; their prolixity is their chief attraction. To this class belong the public speaker's *I am here to tell you, in this day and age* and *at this point in time*, which is becoming a favourite cliché with speakers who find the word *now* rather tame.

We may get an exaggerated idea of the popularity of such clichés because they are especially frequent in the mouths of politicians and others being interviewed on radio or television and fighting for time to think of replies to embarrassing questions. A high-sounding scientific cliché was used by a speaker in reply to a charge that he had exaggerated the number of his supporters: 'We have to study the behaviour patterns.'

Meaningless expletives such as *in fact, you see* and *you know* can become habits and are used far more frequently than the speakers realise. They are frequent in the speech of foreigners, who no doubt think of them as characteristic of colloquial English and deliberately try to acquire them. A German girl who spoke good English had one or two *you knows* in every sentence. An English dramatist interviewed on television provoked one listener to write to a newspaper to point out that he had used the expression *I mean* forty-six times in a fifteen-

minute interview. Another correspondent played the game
rather differently by counting the number of occurrences of the
words *I mean* within a single sentence; his highest score was five.

Prolixity is another individual characteristic. A public
speaker who wished to make a short speech began by saying
that profundity and wit are given to only a few but conciseness
is within the reach of all. This is not strictly true. The ability
to make a simple statement and leave it at that is really rather
rare, and we probably all find that the form in which ideas
come to us is at first needlessly prolix. It was no idle paradox
that caused an author to say that he had written a long book
because he hadn't time to write a short one. An extempore
sermon is often a repetitive one, and a young clergyman who
boasted to his bishop that he had vowed never to use notes
received the unexpected reply 'I absolve you from your vow'.
Many sentences and most books could be shortened with
advantage, but the quest for conciseness can go too far. In
a world in which prolixity and repetition are the rule, a man
who insists too rigidly on saying things once only is liable to
find himself little heeded, and the teacher especially finds it
convenient to acquiesce in the maxim 'What I tell you three
times is true'.

People vary a good deal in the extent to which they tolerate
repetition of commonplace remarks. An elderly housekeeper
whose employer protested at the repetition of a trivial anecdote
some hundreds of times over a period of years replied indignantly: 'It's the first time I've said it today.'

There are some people whose conversation seems to consist
largely of apologies for trivial offences. Such apologies are out
of place in both speech and writing, since it is usually an easy
matter to correct the fault for which one is apologising. A substandard cliché in letters is 'Please excuse scribble'. Such
appeals rarely receive any reply, but a reasonable one would
be: 'On what grounds?' Illegible handwriting shows a lack of
respect for one's correspondent, and the apology merely shows
that the offence is deliberate. Another, less obvious, apology is
incidentally, which is often used as an apology for irrelevance.
A writer using the word should ask himself whether his argument would not be strengthened by the omission of the remark

thus incidentally introduced. Some apologies are really complaints, and the words 'I suppose that I owe you an apology' are often the prelude to an orgy of recrimination and self-justification.

Travellers in a foreign country soon find the need to become familiar with expressions of courtesy. On bumping into a stranger in the corridor of a train, it is a matter of urgency to find some way of letting him know that you have not done it on purpose, and it is equally desirable to have some way of letting a stranger know that his apology is accepted. Books of etiquette often give linguistic hints. One article in an American magazine suggested, reasonably, that it is more courteous to say 'Have a cookie' than 'Have another cookie'. Variations in courtesy very quickly become matters of class dialect. What is technically an apology can become a command, as when 'Pardon!' is used with the meaning 'Say that again'.

Not many people even try to speak the exact truth on all occasions. The motives for departing from the truth may be excellent; the most common is a desire to avoid hurting the feelings of the person they are speaking to. Ellipsis plays a part in replies to conventional questions. An affirmative reply to the question 'Have you got everything you want?' means 'I have everything that it would be reasonable to ask you to supply'. The reply 'I haven't time' means 'What you want me to do is so unimportant to me that I don't intend to spend any time on it'. The answer 'I have my reasons' is generally accepted as equivalent to a refusal to give them, but it was used inappropriately by an old lady who revoked at whist and was asked why she had not followed suit.

Some elliptic replies have become conventional courtesies. 'Lady Dedlock is not at home' means 'Lady Dedlock does not wish to see you'. C. E. M. Joad chose to misunderstand a porter who tried to prevent him from leaving a train at an unscheduled halt: 'This train doesn't stop at this station!' 'That's all right. I'm not on it.' What the porter said was capable of being interpreted as a falsehood, and the passenger called attention to the fact by a reply that was also demonstrably untrue.

The insincerities of everyday life are a frequent subject of satire in plays and novels, and complete candour is often

represented as an amusing and attractive eccentricity. It is
clear that one of the chief attractions of Jane Eyre for Rochester
is her habit of speaking the truth even at the risk of giving
offence. Somerset Maugham's short story *Jane* is about a
middle-aged woman who becomes a great social success by
speaking the truth. Maugham is exercising a novelist's privilege
in exaggerating the popularity which may be gained in this
way, but Catherine Morland in *Northanger Abbey* seems to most
readers an attractive character because of her naïve honesty.

Some people confer favours unobtrusively while others call
attention to the magnitude of the favour that they are con-
ferring, and it is easy to recognise the linguistic practices by
which these different results are achieved. We have all met the
person who makes heavy weather of a trivial offer, thereby
making it almost impossible to accept it: 'Now, if you'd like
milk in your tea, please don't hesitate to mention it. It won't
be a bit of trouble for my husband to get the car out and drive
to the farm for some more milk. . . .' The same desire to call
attention to one's own generosity is found in the stock comic
character, the charwoman who declares herself 'willing to
oblige on Thursdays'. One prospective employer showed her
resentment at such a declaration by saying, in her own class
dialect, 'What I was hoping for was daily condescension.'

Expressions of politeness soon lose their original force when
used insincerely and they can finally become offensive. An
imperative does not now become more acceptable if it is preceded by *Kindly* or *Be so good as to*, though the original motive
for the use of such phrases was to soften the imperative. Another
word that fails of its effect is *respectfully*, when used to describe
one's own conduct. A man who says *I respectfully decline* protests too much; he realises that his refusal may seem discourteous
but he is still determined to refuse. He would do better to let
others decide whether he is being respectful or not. Similarly,
some members of committees make excessive use of the legal
cliché *with respect*, using it to preface every contribution that
they make to the discussion. At best it is unnecessary; at worst
it is an acknowledgement that the remark contains offence of
which nobody but the speaker would otherwise have been
conscious. We have all been taught that there are occasions
when we ought to say 'Please', but to emphasise the word by

extra stress in speech or by underlining it in writing makes a request more rather than less discourteous. Emphasis means that we think that the person addressed would be insensitive to a less emphatic request.

The attempt to teach children good manners can have unfortunate results. The injunction not to accept proffered sweets with an eagerness that may seem greedy can result in an acceptance that seems off-hand or ungracious. 'I don't mind' and 'I'm not particular' are conventional formulas used by children in an attempt to improve on 'Yes, please!' Children became adept at obeying the letter of the injunction not to ask while making their meaning quite clear. A longing look at the desired object or a few words of praise are usually enough to elicit an offer.

It is often felt, and not only in English, that the use of personal pronouns, especially those of the second person, is discourteous. There is a similar reluctance to use the pronoun *I*, a reluctance which may be reinforced by a feeling that excessive use of the first personal pronoun is egotistical. In fact it is less egotistical to say 'I think that this is good' than 'This is good', and to emphasise the pronoun is least egotistical of all, since such emphasis makes it clear that the speaker recognises that others may have different views. In order to avoid the use of the pronoun *I* some people say *one*, which can be regarded as a feature of class dialect. It is most often used by members of the upper classes with intellectual interests, and to other people it is liable to seem an affectation. Historians who wish to make special claims grounded on their historical knowledge are liable to say 'A historian thinks . . .' rather than 'I think . . .' Editors and royal personages use *we* instead of *I*. Ernest Bramah's Kai Lung says *this person* for *I*, but this is a mannerism used to create a foreign atmosphere and not intended to be taken seriously.

The word *yes* is under fire from several directions. One is a matter of pronunciation: [e] is replaced by a wide variety of vowels, the most common of which is [ə]. Forms without a final consonant are common. These may perhaps be derived from the now archaic *yea* and do not necessarily have the ironical or incredulous overtones of 'Oh yeah'. The brevity of the word *yes* makes it unpopular with some speakers, and it is sometimes replaced by *definitely*, *indeed*, *precisely*, *quite*, and *quite so*. These variants are used by different classes of speakers. *Definitely* is for the young; *precisely*, *quite* and *quite so* for the elderly. *Indeed* must be pronounced with enthusiastic intonation if the speaker wishes to express agreement; otherwise it expresses scepticism. It is no doubt courtesy which accounts for the widespread reluctance to use the word *no*. There are various ways of toning down disagreement. One of these is 'Up to a point', but the most common phrase is 'Not really'.

There is constant inflation in the use of expressions of courtesy. *Thank you* becomes *Thank you very much* and later *Thank you very much indeed*. Careful observers are watching with interest for the next stage. A guest expressed his appreciation of a day's entertainment by saying that he had never in his life had such a marvellous day. After he had left, his host quoted this remark with the comment 'Well, I mean, he couldn't have said much less than that, could he?'

In conversation it is usually possible to tell whether those taking part are understanding one another, but the public speaker and the journalist are often denied this satisfaction. Violent agreement or disagreement may result in applause or booing or letters to the editor, but the usual reaction is silence. Hence there is a good deal of unsuspected misunderstanding, which may be revealed by a chance remark. One woman was heard to say that she didn't agree with all this talk about the Common Market. This might have been interpreted as opposition to the proposal that Britain should seek to enter the European Economic Community, but the speaker went on to support her case by saying that there was a very nice market at Fleetwood. She had misunderstood both words, assuming that *common* was a term of abuse and that *market* was a building where goods were offered for sale on stalls, an important feature of the life of many northern towns.

Misunderstandings of words and phrases are more common than is generally realised. Sometimes the hearer thinks that he understands what is said but attributes the wrong meaning to it; sometimes he is not quite sure but keeps quiet because he is ashamed of his uncertainty. Such misunderstandings are especially common when taboos are involved. Schoolboys reading Shakespeare often have very vague or inaccurate ideas about the meaning of words like *incest* or *bastard*; they know that such words are connected with 'the facts of life' but they know that they will cause embarrassment if they ask for precise definitions. The attempt to avoid embarrassment by the use of euphemisms can lead to obscurity. Social workers who referred to *social diseases* found that their hearers did not always know that they were talking about venereal disease. Certain words have acquired derogatory associations, and they are used as mere terms of abuse without sufficient attention being paid to their exact meaning. There is a tendency to feel that one can dispose of an argument by simply gasping out a derogatory abstract noun, and we too often find that the quite legitimate process of editing is described as censorship or punishment as victimisation. Humour is a frequent cause of misunderstanding, the more so when it is of the deadpan kind, whose chief appeal for those who indulge in it is the failure of the person addressed to understand the joke. Academics are particularly fond of self-mockery, which leads them to anticipate opposition by presenting their views in a deliberately exaggerated or absurd form.

A reply whose relevance becomes clear only after a moment's reflection can be more effective than a plain statement of fact. Of this kind was the reply of an American fire-brigade chief, who justified his decision not to rescue a cat from a tree: 'Did you ever see the skeleton of a cat up a tree?' Similarly, in argument a slightly ludicrous analogy may make a stronger appeal to the average man than a syllogism, as in the illustration used to support the view that a man's nationality should depend on his parentage rather than his place of birth: 'There are those who claim that if a kitten is born in an oven, it is a biscuit.'

Euphemisms quickly lose their euphemistic force and so pass out of use to be replaced by others. Several synonyms may continue in use simultaneously. A homosexual may be known as *a pansy, a fairy, a queen, a queer, a poof, a faggot, a consenting adult* or *one of those*. A water closet may be known as *the W.C., the loo, the lavatory, the toilet* or, by a piece of sophisticated self-mockery, *the euphemism*. A phrase is often preferred to a single word, and so we have *the smallest room. Let me show you the geography of the house*, and *Would you like to wash your hands?*

used to refer to what is often described as *a call of nature*. A visitor to a college was once heard to say indignantly: 'I'll never go there again. I told them that I wanted to wash my hands and they showed me into a room with twenty-four wash-basins.'

To the number of ideas which attract euphemisms, we must add any reference to age. It has been said that women are young, middle-aged or wonderful, and for both sexes *middle-aged* is used to describe an age well past the middle of one's life. *Elderly* is preferred to *old*. *Senior citizen* is clearly euphemistic and it shows signs of being killed by ridicule. It is hard to say whether *O.A.P.* as a term for an old-age pensioner is an attempt to gloss over the reference to old age or the result of a wish to curtail a lengthy phrase. People are not only sensitive about being old; they don't like to be reminded that they are young, and it is best not to describe children as children in their presence. An inquiry about the age at which children begin to object to being called children produced the reply that one boy of five had protested indignantly 'I'm not a child; I'm David', but this was perhaps a precocious assertion of individuality rather than a protest against the use of the particular term *child*. Initials are frequently used euphemistically, as in *M.D.* (mentally deficient), *E.S.N.* (educationally subnormal) and *G.B.H.* (grievous bodily harm). In all these examples initials serve the double purpose of achieving euphemism with conciseness.

The use of euphemisms can lead to the growth of a kind of secret language, which is perfectly intelligible to those who are in the know but which can be puzzling to those who are not. It is sometimes necessary to explain to foreigners that a *special area* is not especially attractive and that a boy who has attended an *approved school* is not necessarily better educated than one who has not.

In the Victorian period, when English linguistic taboos were stronger than they are today, distinctions were made according to the sex of the speaker. Certain words were forbidden to both sexes, but some mild oaths, euphemistic in origin, were permitted to men but not to women. A chorus in *The Gondoliers* emphasises the distinction: the men sing 'Don't be so deucedly condescending', while the women sing 'Don't be so dreadfully condescending'. Certain bodily functions were completely taboo, but others, such as sweating, might be mentioned by men but not by women, a convention which gave rise to the famous rebuke: 'Horses sweat; men perspire; young ladies glow.'

Euphemisms are not confined to any one social class. Within the same week B.B.C. programmes presented two interviews. One was with a highly placed official, who replied to an interviewer's question 'Will people be sacked?' by saying 'There will be some redundancies'. The second interview was with a group of office cleaners who were asked how they would like their job to be described. One of the suggestions was *lady help*. The cleaners were united in their dislike of the term *charlady*, thus illustrating the common fate of euphemisms, since the earlier meaning of *charlady* was a lady who undertakes a piece of work of any kind. The general term was specialised to refer to a kind of work that people preferred not to specify, just as the word *undertaker* was specialised to refer to an occupation that people preferred not to mention. The second element of *charlady* is another euphemism, since one of the things that make the English language so difficult is that it is quite all right to call a man a man, but you have to be very careful before calling a woman a woman. The term *charwoman* was not even mentioned by the cleaners who were interviewed, but many people find it even more offensive than *charlady*. The Situations Vacant column of a daily paper shows that domestic service produces a rich crop of euphemisms. People do not often advertise nowadays for a domestic servant; they get better results if they advertise for a helper in the home or a domesticated person. It is natural that war should produce a crop of euphemisms. Money spent in preparation for war is called *defence expenditure*. A future war is described as an *emergency*. Small wars are *local operations*.

A euphemism may have a literary source that is unknown to most of the people who use it. The use of *little Mary* as a childish euphemism for 'stomach' is the main theme of an early and deservedly forgotten play by J. M. Barrie, *Little Mary* (1903), but in the first half of the present century the expression was used by many people who had no knowledge either of the play or of J. M. Barrie.

It is not only improper words that are subject to taboos. A suffix may come to be regarded as derogatory. In the early years of the present century it was usual to describe the inhabitants of Asia as *Asiatics*, but since the Second World War *Asian* has become more usual. Within the last few decades *Empire* and *Colonies*, with their adjectives *imperial* and *colonial*, have become words that are unobtrusively avoided. The Crown Agents for the Colonies have become the Crown Agents for Overseas Governments and Administrations, and the British Empire has become the Commonwealth. To some extent, of course, this is more than a difference of terminology; the change of ideas that makes certain words unfashionable may effect changes in the organisations that are represented by those names. There are obstacles to change. However unpopular the word *Empire* may become, there are large numbers of holders of the orders O.B.E. and M.B.E. who find nothing offensive in it, and the Imperial Tobacco Company and Imperial Chemical Industries are proud survivors of a time when *Imperial* was a term of praise.

Euphemisms are frequently used in the Houses of Parliament in order to avoid the use of unparliamentary language, which would be ruled out of order. When Winston Churchill was a young man, he made use of an example which has become famous. In reply to a suggestion that certain forms of Chinese labour employed in South Africa were no better than slavery, he replied: 'It cannot in the opinion of His Majesty's Government be classified as slavery in the extreme acceptance of the word without some risk of terminological inexactitude.'[1] Churchill in later life had reason to complain that the phrase was used against him as though it were a mere synonym for *lie*. A terminological inexactitude is not just a lie. It is something much more common: a statement which is true only if we give to one of the words used a meaning which cannot be defended. We have now discovered other ways of calling a man a liar. A recent method is to talk about *the credibility gap*.

To describe many groups of people we have pairs of words, both of them generally understood but not interchangeable. One word of the pair is widely used but disrespectful; the other is more formal and tends to be used by the members of the

[1] Ivor Brown, *Mind your Language!* (Bodley Head, 1962) p. 22.

group described by the term. The general public may speak of *parsons*, *bookmakers* and *undertakers* but on more formal occasions they would be described as *clergymen*, *turf accountants* (or *commission agents*) and *funeral directors*. Sometimes the more formal terms make distinctions that are not made in everyday speech. A Nonconformist parson may be described as a *minister of religion* while an Anglican is a *clerk in holy orders*. It is not only names of occupations that are treated in this way; the game which the unregenerate think of as *ping-pong* is known more formally as *table tennis*, a *mouth organ* is a *harmonica*, while the pointed heels of ladies' shoes, fashionable in the sixties and good for lawns but bad for polished floors, were known to the general public as *stiletto heels* but to some of those who sold and wore them as *spindle heels*.

The same characteristic may be described in very different ways according to the light in which the speaker wishes to present the subject. One must admire the loyal wife who said that she sometimes wished that her husband was not always so splendidly firm, whilst realising that many wives would have simply said that he was as stubborn as a mule. Deliberately loaded language is often used in novels and plays with humorous intent. An example is 'Your father was *not* sulking. He was wounded and a little quiet.'[1]

It is not only unpleasant ideas that have to be glossed over; some ideas are thought to be too sacred to be mentioned on trivial occasions. This is the chief reason why some people object to swearing. As a concession to these objections, words with religious associations are often maltreated when used as oaths. *God* becomes *gosh*, and *damn* becomes *darn* or *dash*; *God blind me!* becomes *Gorblimey!* and *God rot it!* becomes *Drat it!* Orthodox Jews are particularly anxious to avoid profane use of the name of God. One Jewish student even wrote of Æsculapius as the 'g–d of medicine' on the grounds that it would be improper to write the word *god* in full, even when it referred to a Greek god. This seems to be carrying the ecumenical approach too far.

Words referring to sexual intercourse or excrement are often used as oaths, though they are likely to cause offence if

---

[1] Kenneth Horne, *Yes and No* (Samuel French, 1937) Act II, scene ii.

used outside a homogeneous group; within such a group they are likely to pass unnoticed. There are dangers in bribing children not to use such words. A small boy who had been promised sixpence if he avoided using a particular word for a week startled his parents by announcing one day: 'I know a word that's worth half a crown.' The word may not have been very bad. Children have their own taboos which do not very much shock their elders. A shocked child reproved a visitor for using the word *stomach* instead of *tummy*.

The extent to which one swears is largely a matter of individual preference. Some people never swear at all; others swear only when deeply moved; and others swear all the time. The sort of swear-word that one chooses is determined partly by class dialects with rapidly changing fashions. Bob Acres, in *The Rivals*, declared that 'Damns have had their day'; today we might have to say the same of bloodies, since the word *bloody* has lost much of the power to shock that it once possessed, but there are large social groups where the word still has a wide currency. By allowing Eliza Doolittle to use the word in *Pygmalion* (1912), Shaw caused a tremendous sensation, and audiences find it hard to pay proper attention to the scene in which the word is used because they are waiting with such rapt attention for the heroine to say 'Not bloody likely'. At one cinema the advertisement of the film version of the play included the information: 'The great moment of the film occurs at 3.15 p.m., also at . . .' The word is now much less offensive than it used to be; its chief function is to add mild emotional colouring to what one is saying, and the chief objection to its frequent use is that it shows a straining after effect rather than that it is an offence against public morals. The chief linguistic interest of the taboo on *bloody* is its arbitrariness. The word does not belong to any of the recognised categories which are generally the subject of euphemism. The theory that *bloody* is from *by our Lady*, and therefore the subject of a religious taboo, has little to recommend it.

Certain oaths have become old-fashioned. The cartoonist Low did much to associate *Gad, sir!* with his Colonel Blimp, and the euphemistic *dashed* is similarly dated. Three public schoolboys who, in 1967, wrote a letter to a newspaper expressing an old-fashioned point of view, showed their recognition of this fact by describing themselves as 'three dashed supporters of the British raj'.

It happens that many of the words which the dictionaries describe as 'not now in polite use' are words of four letters, and in recent years the term *four-letter word* has come into use to describe words of this kind. The use of the term in this sense was almost certainly unfamiliar to the organisers of a competition, held under the most respectable auspices, who invited members to see how many words they could write in a square inch. It was clearly desirable to find some way of avoiding the injustices that would arise from the varying length of words, and it was therefore stipulated that all the words should be four-letter words. Such words always cause trouble to the compilers of dictionaries, and Dr Johnson replied coldly to a lady who congratulated him on having omitted them from his Dictionary by saying 'You have evidently been looking for them, madam'.

The aim of the man who swears is to gain additional emphasis. Bad language is not the only way of achieving this effect. Certain phrases are used solely with the intention of 'piling it on'. Examples are: *looking for all the world like, I cannot for the life of me understand, a cool million* and *there was I*. Such phrases, like swearwords, become meaningless and tiresome with over-use.

Many figures of speech, beside euphemisms, enter into our everyday language, the most common figure being metaphor. Many of the metaphors that are in daily use are dead in that neither speaker nor hearer is conscious that they are metaphors at all, because the etymology has been forgotten. It is pedantry to insist that a heathen must live on a heath or an urbane man in a city, but it is well to avoid metaphors in a context where the etymology, if known, will confront the hearer or the reader with ludicrous associations. Most of the metaphors in everyday use are clichés whose meaning is understood without a very careful examination of the appropriateness. A man will say cheerfully that he has a memory like a sieve and it is most likely that both he and his hearers will take this to mean that he has a bad memory, because a sieve allows things to pass through it. But a sieve does not allow everything to pass through; it holds back certain things and allows the rest to pass through, and that is exactly what a well-trained memory does.

A vivid succession of images can produce an incongruous mixture of metaphors. If a speaker says he smells a rat, that is enough imagery for one sentence, and if he goes on to say that he sees it floating in the air but that he will nip it in the bud, he has weakened the sense instead of strengthening it. Deliberately to avoid the use of metaphor would weaken the language, but it is quite a useful exercise to try from time to time to express in non-figurative language the ideas that are usually clothed in metaphors. For example, in the preceding sentence 'clothed' would become 'expressed'. The exercise is particularly useful in the description of language. What do we mean when we talk about a soft *g* or an open syllable? In linguistics, as in other matters, personal prejudices dictate one's choice of metaphor. Those who dislike loan-words speak of a language that makes use of its own resources as 'pure'; those who like them describe them as 'enriching' the language. In this context 'pure' and 'enrich' are question-begging words.

Many people use figurative language without realising that they are doing so, and are liable to be pulled up short if their hearers, either innocently or mischievously, interpret their words literally. W. S. Gilbert is said to have soothed a woman who complained that she had been described as 'no better than she should be' by saying 'Of course. How could you be?' A professor who warned a student that he was spending too much time on wine, women and song was not completely reassured by the reply 'Very well, I'll stop singing immediately'.

Figurative language can be used to distort the realities of a situation. A student, told that if he did no work and attended no lectures he would be reported as unsatisfactory, replied indignantly: 'Of course, if you are going to hold a pistol to my head. . . .' The metaphor was a reasonable one in that the professor, like a highwayman, was using threats, but the student had introduced a number of new elements into the situation which enabled him to regard himself as the victim of unprovoked aggression, deserving of sympathy rather than blame. The cartoonist's habit of personifying countries as human beings like John Bull or Uncle Sam can lead to false analogies, since we all tend to sympathise with a little man in conflict with a big one and there is therefore a tendency to assume that the smaller a minority group is, the more likely it is to be in the right.

Hyperbole is a common figure of speech in both literature and conversation. The classical instance of hyperbole is that used by the man who claimed that he had been kept awake by the noise made by thousands of cats, but after cross-examination he said: 'Well, anyway, I'm sure that there was our cat and another.' Children take hyperbole for granted, whether used by themselves or by others. A child, interviewed on the radio, said 'I have hundreds of millions of dresses'. The interviewer said 'How many, really?' and the child, without any consciousness of inconsistency between her two estimates, replied 'Four'.

The degree of vigour with which people express their opinions is something that cuts across most class or occupational divisions. It may be that those who have been expensively educated have been taught not to be too ready to express their opinions on any subject to strangers, but when they are together with others belonging to the same social class, some will express their views forcibly and others timidly at every social level. Academics are generally thought to be more ready than most people to weigh all the evidence before expressing an opinion, but even among them one soon learns to recognise those whose contributions to a discussion begin 'I feel very strongly' and those who begin 'I should have thought'. Assessments of the weather are notoriously subjective. A shower of rain may be described as 'raining cats and dogs' or 'just a Scotch mist' according to whether one does or does not want to go out.

Some frequently used expressions are hardly ever true. One such expression is 'It stands to reason', which is often used to buttress an assertion in whose making reason has played little part. Another is 'It's as simple as that'. These words are most often used by those who are laying claim to a larger share of the national cake than others are disposed to allow them, and the phrase serves as a useful warning that the case that has been presented should be carefully examined to make sure that competing claims have been properly considered.

The practice of mentally paraphrasing a claim or an accusation in order to find what is the real meaning of a heavily loaded phrase is a salutary one, especially when one is reading the correspondence column of a newspaper. When a correspondent complains that somebody or other has failed to show effective leadership, he generally means that someone in an official position has failed to share his own prejudices on some controversial issue. One journalist amused himself by translating into idiomatic English some of the phrases used in the letters exchanged when politicians are encouraged to resign. He suggested that 'I have had to make some alterations in the Government rather earlier than I expected' means 'You thought you would get me out first, didn't you?' He translated 'Best wishes for your future' as 'I don't wish you any harm so long as you don't start trying to give trouble', whereas 'Best wishes for your future career' means 'With all those directorships you've got lined up, I'm really doing you a good turn' (*Observer*, 1 May 1966).

4

Registers

THERE are some varieties of language which can be associated neither with groups nor individuals but with the occasions when they are used. These varieties are called registers, and their importance in speech is at last beginning to be recognised. Their study may be regarded as the examination of language in the context within which it is used.

The context in which a word is used has an effect on the meaning that is usually taken for granted. A favourite word in stamp auctioneers' advertisements is 'important'. The man who does not collect stamps probably thinks that this is the last word that he would use to describe a collection of stamps, but the compiler of the advertisement knows that he is writing for collectors, who admit the distinction between an important and an unimportant collection. A man who has broken his collar-bone while hunting may be said to be comfortable and his condition described as satisfactory. One would have thought that only the fox could derive any satisfaction from the condition of a huntsman with a broken collar-bone, and the patient himself would probably regard 'comfortable' as a singularly ill-chosen word, but the words are chosen not by the patient but by those who are looking after him, who have their own standards of comparison. As a result of frequent use in a particular kind of context, words change their meanings, and such a change is affecting the word 'satisfactory'. Students who have been told that their essays are satisfactory sometimes ask indignantly what is wrong with them.

Some words and phrases occur in more than one context with a difference of meaning. For some people Easter is primarily a religious festival, while for others it is primarily a bank holiday, and the two groups give a different meaning to the phrase *Easter Saturday*. Those for whom Easter is primarily a religious festival think of Easter week as beginning with Easter

Sunday, and for them Easter Saturday is the Saturday of Easter week, i.e. the Saturday after Easter Sunday. Those who think of Easter as first and foremost a holiday think of Easter Saturday as the day before Easter Sunday, one of the days in a holiday weekend.

The invention of the telephone has introduced a new register to the English language. Certain sounds which are quite distinct in ordinary speech seem alike when heard on the telephone. For this reason users of the telephone are officially exhorted to mispronounce certain words in order to avoid confusion. It has been found that on the telephone *five* is liable to be confused with *nine*, and subscribers are therefore urged to replace the second consonant of *five* by [f]. Trilling of the consonant [r] does not come naturally to most speakers of English, but in asking for a number they are asked to trill their *r*'s for the sake of distinctness. Distinctness is particularly necessary when one is asking for a number, since the hearer is deprived of the help provided by context, which is much greater than most people realise. To test this theory it is only necessary to try pronouncing the word *glad* as [dlæd]. Very few people will notice the substitution of [d] for [g], because they are expecting [g] and there is no word *dlad* in English. The extended use of automatic dialling is making obsolete much of the advice about asking for a number, but similar problems occur in telephone conversations. A speaker on the telephone is deprived of the help of gesture and facial expressions and he tends to speak more loudly than necessary. Probably most people can tell by ear alone whether a speaker whose voice they overhear in the next room is using the telephone or not.

If automatic dialling has done much to lessen the importance of one register, broadcasting has introduced another. It is often said that radio and television are removing the last traces of regional dialect from English speech, but the English used by speakers in radio programmes is less homogeneous than is sometimes supposed. The B.B.C. has brought daily programmes in standard English to large numbers of people who might otherwise have spent their lives hearing little but regional dialect, but it is not certain that it has had much influence on the speech of those who listen to it. There are large numbers of people who listen to radio news bulletins every day but who would be acutely embarrassed at the suggestion that they should talk like that. Even B.B.C. announcers do not talk alike, and in the programmes as a whole there is even greater diversity of speech. In the various magazine programmes large numbers of people are interviewed speaking a wide variety of local and class dialects. What the B.B.C. has done has been to make available a wide range of varieties of English for those who wish to study them. The Queen's Christmas broadcasts have given to the phrase *the Queen's English* a reality which, for most of her subjects, it did not previously possess. The B.B.C. has a department to advise announcers on variant pronunciations, especially of proper names, and in the 1920s it had a distinguished advisory committee, but it does not seek to impose uniformity. There is therefore no point in the frequently heard comment that a particular pronunciation is 'used regularly by speakers employed by the B.B.C.'.

Apart from pronunciation, speakers on the radio, especially in news bulletins, have begun to develop their own register. One form of words frequently used to conclude a programme is: 'And so, until tomorrow evening, it's from us goodbye.' We have learnt to recognise the slight pause with which they indicate that what follows is a quotation. One feature of syntax is the use of the conjunction *and* to link the title of an item with the first sentence. Examples are:

Northern Ireland, and the Government have agreed to an inquiry.

Bolivia, and it is now clear that . . .

Malta, and the British Government has rejected . . .

Cricket, and play resumed at Headingley this morning.

Vietnam, and here is our own correspondent.

Another habit of interviewers is to put a question into the third person addressed to the listener, but the person interviewed answers it as though it were addressed to him, as, in fact, it probably was before the editor of a tape-recording got to work. We thus get announcers saying 'How does Mr Blank see this problem?'

The technique of interviewing has affected the meaning of the word *live* [laiv]. A recent press announcement gave the news that the Prime Minister would shortly be interviewed live from Downing Street on television. A reader a century ago would have been inclined to ask what other sort of interview is possible, but a reader of today recognises the implicit distinction between an interview that is broadcast when it takes place and one which is recorded and possibly edited.

In carrying out their perfectly proper function of making an incoherent statement intelligible, interviewers are sometimes patronising. Clumsy expression is only one of the causes of lack of clarity; another is that the speaker is trying to express shades of meaning of which a less subtle interviewer may be quite unconscious. Henry James is said to have suffered a good deal in conversation from people who finished his sentences for him with words that he had rejected as inadequate to express his exact meaning. A radio interviewer will often say 'What you are trying to say is . . .' One woman being interviewed replied coldly: 'I hope I was succeeding.' One can sometimes hear a person interviewed trying to gain time for thought by saying patronisingly 'That's a very good question'. It must be a great temptation to the interviewer to reply 'I know. Will you answer it?' The great weakness of most interviews is that the interviewer is so anxious to avoid boring listeners that, unless the person interviewed is a celebrity, he is given no time to say anything worth saying. It is always refreshing to notice the sudden change of tone when a speaker's interest is really aroused. One woman gave predictable replies to the offer of two packets of an unnamed brand of a commodity in exchange for one packet of an advertised brand. When assured that the offer was a genuine one, she lapsed into the vernacular: 'Are you on the level or are you just mucking about?'

Most games have their own technical vocabulary used and understood all over the country and forming a part of the standard language, but this standard technical vocabulary is supplemented by other groups of words which may belong to regional dialects or slang. Mr J. L. Bailes has written an article showing how varied is the vocabulary of the game of marbles.[1] In a game of bowls, one of the players said 'It's got no legs but it will do for a policeman'. This sounds like a slander on a splendid body of men, but a wood with no legs is one that is propelled with insufficient force so that it stops some distance short of the jack. A policeman is a wood which performs useful service by getting in the way of one's opponent. Such terminology can become very familiar to those who habitually play a particular game, and can become a semi-secret language. Many bridge-players have, in flagrant defiance of the rules of the game, given a warning to their partners: 'There's many a man.' To an outsider this warning is meaningless, but a player who has moved in circles where habits were not austere knows that it means 'There's many a man walking the streets of London without a penny in his pockets because he didn't get trumps out soon enough'.

It is not only in universities that the importance of accuracy and precision is emphasised. A policeman, giving evidence, soon learns the importance of distinguishing between observation and inference, and in military intelligence similar caution is necessary. On a parade ground, where it is important that movements should be synchronised, there is a great need for monosyllabic words of command. If they don't exist, they must be created by giving an unnatural stress and tempo to existing polysyllabic words. A drill sergeant who believed that *attention* should be stressed on the second syllable would get nowhere. For him it is stressed on the final syllable, which is preceded by a pause which serves the purpose of warning the hearers to be on the alert to listen for the final word of instruction. However much clichés are frowned upon in other registers, in military use they are invaluable. The soldier learns to respond instantly to a particular auditory stimulus, and there is no place for elegant variation. The officer cadet who said 'Fire on my instructions!' instead of 'Await my order to fire!' found that there are real advantages in deferring the word 'fire' until the end of the sentence, thus avoiding the burst of rifle fire with which well-trained recruits respond to the word when it is used without preamble. That imperatives should be common in the

[1] 'A Vocabulary of Marbles', *Transactions of the Yorkshire Dialect Society*, XLVIII (1948) 12–23.

language of the armed forces is inevitable, but one feature of such language is the deliberate replacement of the imperative by the future on occasions when speed and synchronisation are not required: 'All ranks will report . . .'

The evidence given in courts of law by police officers is full of stereotyped phrases. There is something to be said for this practice. If a policeman were allowed to speak naturally, those who are accustomed to hear police evidence might think that there was some subtle reason for his departures from the traditional pattern. Similarly, a bridge-player who from time to time varies the form of words that he uses in bidding may be suspected of using a code to convey information to his partner.

Actors, like clergymen, have to learn how to speak loudly and clearly, and they sometimes carry what they have learnt into their everyday life. Visitors to a seaside resort were once regaled with the sight of an elaborately dressed woman saying to the man who accompanied her, in a voice that would have been clearly audible at the back of the pit: 'Now, *he's* different. He recognises mah ability and he loves muh.'

Every examiner in English literature learns to recognise a number of clichés which tend to occur in essays again and again. One examiner's collection is listed by Professor Randolph Quirk:

> lofty flights of imagination; inimitable narrative technique; organic unity; consummate skill; consummate art; heights of majesty; heights of tragedy; inherent atmosphere; essential atmosphere; inherent appeal; essential appeal; essential characteristics.[1]

Any examiner could supplement this list by examples from his own reading. For example, vague adjectives of approval include *fascinating, profound, exciting, stimulating, lively, subtle* and *impressive*. Nouns include *ambiguity* and *symbolism*. Such clichés are the result of requiring candidates to undertake tasks beyond their strength. Literary criticism is a difficult art but proficiency in it is expected from candidates whose natural comments on books that they read would be of the type 'It was all right' or 'It wasn't as bad as I thought it was going to be'. No wonder

---

[1] *The Use of English*, 2nd ed. (Longmans, 1968) p. 250.

that they take the easy way out by assimilating phrases of the kind that seems to be expected and reshuffling them. It is refreshing, though sometimes disconcerting, to find school-children from time to time expressing literary criticism in their own natural idiom. One girl wrote of *Twelfth Night*: 'It is a jolly play and that Malvolio is a swank-pot.' Literary criticism of a more hostile kind was expressed by a schoolboy who said in a resigned tone of voice at the beginning of an English lesson: 'More hey nonny nonny and bloody daffodils.'

An important aspect of register is the modification of speech to indicate our attitude towards the subject under discussion or towards the person we are talking to. This can be done by modifying the pitch, the loudness and the tempo of the voice. We express anger, impatience, sympathy or affection in this way almost every time we open our mouths. Differences in attitude are expressed also by the choice of near-synonyms. For most frequently recurring ideas it is possible to find pairs of words, one indicating approval and the other disapproval. We like people who are *brave* or *thrifty*, but other people may regard them as *foolhardy* or *niggardly*. The use of favourable words to describe our own actions while we reserve unfavourable ones to describe the action of others is a common source of humour in plays and novels. In an attempt to tone down a reproof or to make light of our own offences, we may describe as *naughty* actions which others would describe as *wicked*. Some words are a deliberate appeal to our emotions: *great* and *little* have emotional overtones that are not present in *large* and *small*. There was no doubt about the sympathies of a writer who reported that a young lad had been accused of robbing an old hag. Such emotional appeals do not remain the same from one century to another and they play an influential part in the semantic history of words. *Naughty* did not always have the trivial associations that it has today; as its etymology implies, it originally meant 'worthless'. It has had a divergent development in standard English and regional dialects, where *nowty* now means 'bad-tempered'. Some words are thought of as vulgar or undignified, and our attitudes towards them are similarly unstable. Dr Johnson in his Dictionary attached the label 'low' to *fun* and *clever*. On the other hand, we regard *shove* as an undignified word, but O.E. *scūfan* was used in heroic poetry with no feeling of incongruity. Certain words fall into disesteem as a result of use by people in a subordinate position. A university bursar could not understand the annoyance of a college principal at being asked to 'submit an application'. The bursar was using a phrase that he had used to some thousands of applicants for admission without intending any discourtesy; the principal was equally familiar with the phrase in such a context but did not feel that it should be applied to him.

The woman who replied indignantly 'I am not a good woman' when addressed as 'My good woman' may have expressed herself badly, but her protest was justified. To address either a man or a woman as 'good', especially when the adjective is preceded by the possessive adjective, is offensive because it is patronising; some things should be taken for granted.

When anyone hears his own voice played back to him on a tape-recording machine, he is usually shocked and incredulous. Something must be allowed for the imperfections of mechancial recording, but it is quite common for a speaker to find that his incredulity is not shared by his friends. The conclusion must be that we do not always know how our own voices sound to other people, and our ignorance applies both to the general impression and to details of pronunciation. Probably most of us have found that there are days when everyone that we meet seems to be friendly and other days when everybody seems to be irritable. The most likely explanation is that people are responding to our own mood as expressed in our intonation, which seems to us to be perfectly normal. A similar explanation accounts for much of the dissension between husbands and wives.

Language can reflect the attitude of a speaker to the subject under discussion. Those who, like Ogden Nash, proclaim boldly that the interest they take in their neighbour's nursery would have to grow to be even cursory are liable to reveal this lack of interest by the use of the neuter pronoun *it* when referring to a baby, whose parents prefer to use *he* or *she*, and there is a similar variation between animal-lovers and others in the choice of pronoun when referring to pets. A man who cares little for pets is liable to refer to the cat as 'it'; a lover of animals is more likely to say 'he' or 'she'.

Language is sometimes used to provoke the person addressed. In a civilised society the provocation is rarely direct and extreme. Touchstone distinguished seven degrees in giving an opponent the lie, and today we do not often go beyond the countercheck quarrelsome. In fact, the provocation may not be expressed by the choice of words at all; it may be conveyed by intonation, by a scowl or by a failure to smile in circumstances where a smile might be expected. When words are used, a single word may be enough to express the rage in the speaker's heart. To call one's opponent by the wrong name, suggesting that he is little-known and unimportant, is an old device, but even if the correct name is used, its frequent introduction in public debate can be offensive ('But, Mr Smith, you surely do not mean . . .'). Similarly, the occasional use of 'sir' may be respectful, but its excessive use can be offensive. The frequent use of the word by a young man to a middle-aged man can cause offence, but here the offence is usually unintentional: the older man prefers not to be constantly reminded that he is so obviously getting old when he feels so young. The addition of a single word may show that tempers are wearing thin. 'What is that supposed to mean?' is more offensive than 'What does that mean?' To accuse a man of cowardice is a common way of trying to provoke him, as in 'If that is what he means he should have the guts to say why', but lack of courage is only one of many motives that may discourage a man from giving his reasons. One device that is used, sometimes unconsciously, to express disapproval is to speak with nearly empty lungs. This gives the impression that the speaker is weighed down by an almost intolerable load but is determined to struggle on bravely. Two words often used with a desire to be unpleasant are *so-called* and *exactly*. A reference to 'your so-called university' has been known to produce the mild retort 'Well, what would *you* call it?', and it is a sign that tempers are rising when one of the parties to a conversation says 'Just what do you mean by that?' A question like 'Where exactly do you want to sit?' is not really a demand for precision on a subject in which precision is neither necessary nor attainable; it is merely an indication of a desire to pick a quarrel. Adverbs indicating precision have other uses. Among academics they are used with a negative to avoid making a definite statement, which might seem unscholarly, and their use can become a habit. An examiner who sought to defend a not very good student by saying that at least he expressed his own ideas, met with the reply: 'Well, they aren't exactly his own and they aren't exactly ideas.'

Official language takes several different forms, which fall into two broad divisions: the ceremonial language which deliberately sets out to be different from the language of everyday life, and the language used by civil servants in their communications with one another and with the public. At its best, this kind of English is not recognisable as a distinct variety, but civil servants are open to special linguistic temptations and, if they give way to them, they develop their own variety of English. The eminent civil servant Sir Ernest Gowers wrote his *Plain Words* to warn them against these temptations, and the advice that he gave was so obviously sensible that his book has had a circle of readers much wider than that for which it was originally intended.

Most people find the occasional use of formal and ceremonial language impressive. For example, the words used when a juryman is sworn in give him a sense of the gravity and dignity of the occasion. A good example of ceremonial language is the formula used to forbid brawling during the annual meeting on the Thingwald Hill in the Isle of Man. The words spoken by the Coroner of Glenfala, one of the sheriffs of the island, gain in impressiveness by the use of archaism and repetition:

> I do fence the King of Man and his officers, that no manner of man do brawl or quarrel nor molest the audience, lying, leaning or sitting and to show their accord, and answer when they are called by licence of the King of Man and his officers. I fence this court! I fence this court! I fence this court! I do draw witness to the whole audience that the court is fenced![1]

But such language is not for everyday use. When it became known that the Prince of Wales was to enter the Navy, it was

[1] F. J. Drake–Carnell, *Old English Customs and Ceremonies* (Batsford, 1938) p. 43.

reported in the press that he would be known to his fellow-midshipmen as 'Mr Midshipman, His Royal Highness the Prince of Wales Prince Charles'. The remark of a B.B.C. commentator (28 February 1970) deflated this pomposity with a nice mixture of scepticism and ridicule: 'I'll bet he will.'

As a rule Englishmen are embarrassed by eloquence, but in times of national peril oratory comes into its own, and the war speeches of the Younger Pitt and Winston Churchill satisfied a real need during the Napoleonic Wars and the Second World War. The orator's delivery is naturally louder than that used on more ordinary occasions, and it is also slower; to allow time for the echo to die down the speaker has to pause after each group of words. A skilful orator learns to make good use of variations of speed and loudness to increase the effectiveness of his speech. He may make a similar use of contrast in his choice of words. His normal diction is likely to be more exalted than that of everyday life, but he may relieve the strain on his hearer by the sudden introduction of a piece of slang or colloquialism.

The spread of television has led to the growth of a different type of oratory. The platform orator responds to his audience as much as they to him, but the speaker on television can only guess what effect he is having on his hearers. The result is a speech which makes less of an appeal to mass emotions but more of an appeal to reason, and the manner of delivery is more matter-of-fact, since the speaker is deprived of the intoxicating reaction of a large audience.

Parliamentary oratory is yet a third kind of public speaking that has its own rules, some of them disconcerting to the speaker. Platform oratory is addressed in the main to the speaker's supporters, though he has to learn how to deal with a small number of hecklers. A parliamentary orator, on the other hand, is addressing both supporters and opponents, and his audience is almost entirely made up of practised speakers. If he begins with a provocative remark, he may arouse so much hostility that he gets no hearing. His chief enemy, however, is indifference rather than hostility. He must be prepared for a very small audience, which becomes smaller still as members get up and walk out in the middle of his speech. Many of those who remain do so because they themselves want to make a speech and they are likely to become impatient if they have to listen to a long speech, however good. A pause for effect is dangerous because two or three of his audience may assume that the speech is finished and may be on their feet to catch the Speaker's eye. If important decisions are taken outside Parliament the sense of tension may be removed from parliamentary debates, and sometimes a debater is not really interested in his parliamentary audience but is 'talking for Buncombe', making a speech which will please his electors at home when it is reported in the local press. If he is too witty he is liable to be dismissed as a mere entertainer, and he must not be too anxious to make a 'debater's point', which is irrelevant to the main issue. Most parliamentary proceedings do not lend themselves to oratorical treatment. Questions on departmental matters and the clause-by-clause discussion of bills are carried on in Civil Service language. This is understandable, since replies to questions are usually drafted by civil servants and read aloud by ministers. Traditional courtesy leads to euphemistic phrases. For example, 'This should be treated with the greatest reserve' might be paraphrased 'Don't trust him an inch'.

When oratory is not backed by deep emotion, it becomes the turgid style of the public speaker, which is not confined to Parliament. Strangely enough, the result of being called upon to speak when one has only a sketchy idea of what one wants to say is not silence but prolixity. Only an unusually strong-minded speaker can sit down as soon as he has made his point; too many speakers give way to the temptation to make it again in slightly different words. A device to give the speaker time to think is the use of conventional resounding phrases of little meaning such as 'I am here to tell you', 'in this day and age', 'I think that I may say, without fear of contradiction' or 'This is not the place nor am I the man to enlarge further on this subject'. Phrases such as these are often used in formal public speeches and they can be regarded as signs that the speaker has undertaken a task beyond his strength, but they would seem pompous if used in conversation.

Some pronunciations are much used by public speakers who wish to make their voices carry. The word 'empire' normally has stress on the first syllable but, in the days before it became a dirty word, it was much used by public speakers who, using it

at the end of a sentence, gave additional force and a monoph-
thongal pronunciation to the second syllable. A newspaper
critic of a television programme alluded to this practice when,
referring to Edwardian nostalgia, he used the spelling *Empah*
(*Daily Telegraph*, 24 March 1968).

Official language often reveals a lack of courage. The writer
is afraid to make a plain statement that could be challenged or
that could commit his superiors to action that they might not
be willing to take. A frequent device is to use the conditional to
convey decisions: 'The Minister would scarcely agree.' The
passive voice is often used in official language because there is
some uncertainty about who is supposed to have taken a decision. The conventions of anonymity and collective responsibility often demand that this information should be concealed
from the public. There are also bits of padding like 'for your
information' and 'I must remind you'.

If we may accept the following quotation as accurate, turgid
language can be combined with faulty syntax and its use can
lead to a very healthy revolt:

> A report of the city planning office, dated September 18:
> '. . . there does not appear to be any mitigating circum-
> stances from a planning aspect to justify exceeding a 3:5 plot
> ratio, especially bearing in mind that the hotel and office
> components of the scheme could easily well occupy many
> other sites in the city centre.' It concluded with a recommen-
> dation that permission be refused on the grounds of 1, exces-
> sive plot ratio density; 2, daylight failure; and 3, unsatis-
> factory massing and elevational treatment. The analysis was
> subsequently reduced to more vernacular terms for my
> benefit by a Councillor. 'It means the whole scheme was too
> big, too gloomy and too ugly.'
>
> *Sunday Times*, 13 December 1970

The story of a civil servant who erased his initials from a
memorandum and was then required to initial the erasure has
a logic of its own. Similarly, a logical defence could be brought
forward for the civil servant responsible for the series of minutes
which appeared in one Ministerial file:

Has nothing been done in this case since Jan. 12?
Yes.

What?
Nothing.

This represents the same sort of triumph of logic over usage that causes many people to claim that a double negative is equivalent to an affirmative.

In less exalted government departments there is much use of stereotyped phrases. Quite junior clerks can deal with a situation which consists of identifying a set of frequently recurring circumstances and handing out the appropriate letter which, though typed, is virtually a form.

Government officials have to handle such a vast mass of material that orderly arrangement with much subdivision is necessary to prevent it from getting out of hand, but such habits, once acquired, are not easily lost. The result can be a kind of pedantry which uses pretentious language to describe everyday things. A visitor to a government building in Washington, D.C., found a door with the following imposing sign:

> 4156
> General Services Administration
> Region 3
> Public Buildings Service
> Building Management Division
> Utility Room
> Custodial

On inquiry he discovered that the room in question was a broom cupboard.

In recent years civil servants have tried to free themselves from the traditional style and to write in a more simple and natural way. It is often instructive to compare different editions of leaflets intended for wide circulation to see how the style has changed. The Ministry of Pensions and National Insurance issued a leaflet containing the warning:

> A claimant who loses his employment through misconduct (in its industrial sense) or who leaves his employment voluntarily without just cause may be disqualified for benefit of not more than six weeks.

In later editions this became:

> If you leave your employment voluntarily without just cause
> or lose it through misconduct (in its industrial sense) you
> may be disqualified from benefit for a period of not more
> than 6 weeks.

There is often some uncertainty whether a particular variety of
language is to be associated with an occasion or with a group
of people. When a barrister in a court of law speaks of another
barrister as 'my learned friend', the occasion is important, but
the profession of the speaker is even more so. Judges have
rebuked witnesses for using the phrase, since it is by convention
reserved for the use of lawyers. Amusement is sometimes caused
by the legal practice of using the pronoun 'we' to emphasise
the identity of interests of a lawyer and his client, as when an
obviously prosperous barrister declares: 'We are an undis-
charged bankrupt suing *in forma pauperis*.' The practice lends
itself to parody. The following passage, from a novel dealing
in a light-hearted way with the law, shows the ludicrous effect
of the use of the plural pronoun heightened by a mixture of
registers. A barrister is consulting a colleague:

> Alan, old man, what the hell constitutes indecent exposure?
> We were walking peacefully down Piccadilly in an old pair
> of trousers and they split. It was Sunday: we couldn't dash
> into a shop for succour, we couldn't place a hand over the
> tear without drawing attention to ourself . . . so we did the
> honourable thing and with every sign of good breeding con-
> tinued on our way ignoring what had taken place. So damn
> me if a blasted copper didn't take one look at us and run us
> in: as if anybody would voluntarily walk down Piccadilly
> like that in daytime – and on a Sunday.[1]

The use of common words in a technical legal sense can be
incongruous, as when an 'infant' turns out to be six feet tall.

One legal pronunciation has come to be reflected in spelling:
that of *lord* as *lud*. A judge of the Supreme Court is addressed as
'my Lord' and *O.E.D.* reports (s.v. Lord sb. 15b): 'The hurried or affected pronunciation prevalent in the courts of law has

[1] Hastings Draper, *Wiggery Pokery* (W. H. Allen, 1956) p. 5.

often been derisively represented by the spelling *my Lud* or *m'lud*.' Lawyers firmly adhere to the 'unreformed' pronunciation of the Latin phrases that are used as technical legal terms. In the schoolroom *nisi* may be pronounced [ni:si:], but in the courts it is [naisai].

Judges are often ridiculed for asking what seem to be silly questions. The ridicule is misplaced for two reasons. The first is that the judge is reminding his hearers of the necessity of defining one's terms. The answer to a question like 'What is a motor-car?' may not be as obvious as it appears at first sight. For example, does the term apply to a delivery van? The second justification for a judge's question is that he may know the answer himself but it is his duty to ask a question if he thinks that any of the jury may not share his knowledge. In much the same way a cross-talk comedian who has been asked a question repeats it for the benefit of those members of the audience who are hard of hearing or slow on the uptake.

The translation of the written language of the law into spoken language calls for some technical skill. A television series based on A. P. Herbert's *Misleading Cases* led to a protest from a law student:

> Surely so thorough a litigant as Mr Haddock knows that the 'v' in the name of a civil case is pronounced 'and' and also that, for example, '[1910] 2 K.B. 113' is pronounced, in Court, as 'Reported in the second volume of King's Bench cases for 1910 at page 113'.
>
> *Radio Times*, 10 October 1968

A good deal of the language of the law is of French or Anglo-Norman origin. Sometimes a French word has been introduced as a loan-word with a specialised legal sense. A *puisne judge* is one of junior status (O.F. *puis né*) and the word has survived, with a change of spelling as well as meaning, in the English word *puny*. Their French origin has affected the word-order of a number of legal phrases. In English an adjective usually precedes its noun, but as a result of French influence we have the legal terms *malice prepense* (and its partial translation *malice aforethought*), *court martial* and *heir apparent*.

Some legal terms are frequently misunderstood or misused

in non-legal contexts. *Without prejudice* is often used in the sense 'without bias', and such a sense is reasonable enough, but it invites confusion with the legal meaning of the phrase, which is 'without detriment to an existing right or claim'. *A leading question* is one that is so worded as to suggest a particular reply that the questioner wants to elicit; it is not necessarily an important question, though that is the sense that is sometimes given to it, and it is often used wrongly to describe a question which the person questioned finds it hard to answer. People often speak of *a prescriptive right* as though the adjective strengthened the noun, but it is one based upon long and unchallenged custom and is less, not more, valid than many other kinds of right.

The written varieties of legal English are more widely known than the spoken. With luck it is possible for a man to keep clear of a court of law for the whole of his life, but most of us from time to time see legal documents, such as insurance policies or the deeds of a house. To a layman the most obvious characteristic of legal documents is their prolixity, but there are good reasons for this. Sir Ernest Gowers, who cannot be accused of excessive tenderness towards verbosity, defends that of legal documents:

> It is the duty of a draftsman of these authoritative texts to try to imagine every possible combination of circumstances to which his words might apply and every conceivable misinterpretation that might be put on them, and to take precautions accordingly. He must avoid all graces, not be afraid of repetitions, or even of identifying them by *aforesaids*; he must limit by definition words with a penumbra dangerously large, and amplify with a string of near-synonyms words with a penumbra dangerously small; he must eschew all pronouns when their antecedents might possibly be open to dispute and generally avoid every possible grammatical ambiguity.[1]

A legal document is prolix because its author is trying to secure complete coverage of a given area of meaning, and the style becomes involved as a result of the author's attempt to achieve a precise definition of this area. In ordinary writing we

[1] Sir Ernest Gowers, *The Complete Plain Words* (Penguin Books, 1962) pp. 19–22.

D

are willing to leave out phrases to be supplied by the intelligence and goodwill of the reader, but the lawyer finds it best to take nothing for granted. He is not greatly concerned with graceful style or speed of comprehension; his chief concern is avoidance of ambiguity. Punctuation can lead to ambiguity, and consequently lawyers try to avoid it. Legal documents generally deal with familiar situations, and conventional formulas are freely used. These appeal to a lawyer because, when interpreting them, he is on familiar ground, supported by numerous precedents.

A legal characteristic is the co-ordination of a number of near-synonyms, such as 'altered, modified or transformed', and of singular and plural forms of the same noun, such as 'the Trustees or Trustee'. There are long sentences and intricate systems of cross-reference. The prefixing and suffixing of prepositions is a common feature of legal English, and words like *aforesaid, hereby, hereof, hereunder* and *hereinafter* are freely used. The use of such words is necessary if precision is to be achieved. The fondness of legal draftsmen for these words makes them unsuitable for use in other contexts, because the use of legal-sounding language to a correspondent who is expecting an informal letter suggests that we don't trust him. It is usually an easy matter to replace legal terminology by more colloquial language: *thereof* becomes *of it*, *therein* becomes *in it*, and some of the longer words can be omitted altogether.

Commerce has developed its special varieties of both written and spoken English. Many of the conventional phrases that have given commercial writing a bad name are the result of dictation. When dictating a letter, one is tempted to string together a lot of clichés. Phrases that were originally courteous have, as a result of mechanical repetition, become less courteous than their more straightforward equivalents. A letter becomes 'your esteemed favour'. The recipient of a letter feels it necessary to assure the sender that he has not only received but also read it and he wishes to make it clear that he is not only courteous but also brisk and efficient. His letter therefore begins 'Your esteemed favour to hand and contents noted'. If he is feeling exuberant, he may say that the contents have been duly noted. He may conclude the letter by assuring his correspon-

dent of his 'best attention at all times'. In the course of the
letter the words 'I beg' are liable to recur needlessly and the
same mechanical courtesy explains phrases like 'Enclosed
please find' instead of 'I enclose'. Conventions have grown up
in commercial writing, like that of using *ult.*, *instant* and *prox.*
instead of the names of the last, the current and the next month
respectively.

The use of the second-person pronoun to a comparative
stranger is for some reason often thought to be disrespectful. In
some languages this feeling has led to the use of the third
personal pronoun as a respectful form of the second person. In
commercial English a similar feeling causes some writers of
letters to replace *you* by *your goodself*, with *good* and *self* joined
together as a single word, a practice of which one person
addressed in that way was heard to say that it made him feel
badsick.

Some of the features of commercial English are simply time-
saving devices. It obviously takes time to fill in the dates on a
batch of circulars, so some businessman had the idea of trans-
ferring the responsibility to the post office by using the words
'Date as postmark'. The practice has little to recommend it,
since it calls attention to the writer's unwillingness to take the
trouble to add the date. It is least objectionable when used on a
postcard, since the postmark is not liable to be detached from
the document to which it refers. A clear example of the misuse
of the phrase was its use in a letter from a candidate applying
for admission to a university. He had no doubt seen the phrase
somewhere and thought it looked businesslike.

Some words and phrases that were once in general use have
survived as features of commercial English after becoming
obsolete elsewhere. The use of *the same* as a pronoun is now virtually confined to commercial English as a synonym for the
pronouns *it* or *them*, but it is found in the Thirty-nine Articles:
'The riches and goods of Christians are not common, as touching the right title and possession of the same.'

Some words serve a useful purpose in that they are technical
terms used to describe commercial practices, but they are
liable to be misused. *Pro forma* means '(done) for form's sake',
and the phrase is used with courteous diffidence in commercial
English to describe an invoice which the sender expects to be

paid before the goods are sent, but *pro-forma* is sometimes used nowadays as a synonym for *form*, thus making three syllables grow where one grew before.

Shops have developed their own language. With some of it one can sympathise. Most people feel that it is pedantic to insist that morning gives way to afternoon exactly at noon. For some hours in the middle of the day there is a period which may be called morning or afternoon according to the accident of whether the speaker has had his lunch. Shop assistants save themselves and their customers a lot of trouble by using 'Good day' as a form of greeting or farewell. It is less easy to sympathise with the snobbishness which rejects the everyday name of an everyday object in favour of some less familiar word. A customer who asks for socks is likely to be shown what the shopkeeper describes as hose. A shopkeeper, asked for thick socks, replied disdainfully, 'Ah, you want a pair of working socks.' The word *shop* itself is sometimes avoided as rather vulgar, and in recent years some shopkeepers have begun, without shame, to describe their shops as *boutiques*. Not all shops can be so described: a boutique is usually small and is likely to contain goods with an individual character such as antiques or fashionable clothes. It is not certain whether it is admiration or derision that has led to such imitations as *beautique* for a hairdresser, *boatique* for a ship's chandler, *scootique* for a shop selling scooters and *shoetique* for a boot and shoe shop. Snobbishness usually leads to a reaction, and the term 'the rag trade' is used to describe the business of selling quite expensive clothes.

The two registers of commerce and journalism meet in the language of advertising. The advertiser sees his product through rose-coloured spectacles, and the public for whom he caters gets into the way of making allowance for his optimism. When a restaurant advertises a lunch consisting of 'rich golden-brown sea-food with superfine French fried potatoes as a side-dish', a few moments of thought are needed before the customer realises that what he has been offered is in fact fish and chips. Advertisements offering property for sale have become notorious for their use of genteel euphemisms. If you bang your head whenever you go upstairs it is some consolation to know that you have bought 'a dwelling-house of character'. On toiling up a steep hill to reach the house, you may remember that the advertisement said 'the site is pleasantly elevated', and if you have some difficulty in finding the house at all, that simply confirms the advertiser's statement that it is 'delightfully secluded in a unique "away from it all" position'.

In advertisements inflated language is used to make commonplace products seem glamorous; in public notices it is used to deprive unwelcome announcements of their sting. It would be hard to find a nicer way of informing the public that there won't be so many buses than the notice at a provincial bus-stop:

This service will operate as at present, though on a revised frequency.

One of the wiles of the advertiser is to seek to impress the reader by the use of long words whose meaning he is not likely to understand. The story of the farmer who bought a field on being assured that it was richly megalithic is no doubt untrue, but it would be an easy matter to collect advertisements that give an air of glamour by using long words to describe properties of the product that are either commonplace or disadvantageous. The advertiser relies on the reader's quite reasonable refusal to confine his attention to literal statements of fact. One advertiser is said to have done quite well by inserting an advertisement consisting of the words 'Only another three weeks to send your dollar', followed by his name and address. Advertisements can provide useful material for students of the English language who are interested in the distinction between what is actually said and what is merely suggested. The words 'after consultation with', followed by the name of some eminent person, can give the unwary the impression that the eminent person supported the proposal. In fact he may have been strongly opposed to it, and the proposal may have been made in deliberate contradiction of his views. The statement is literally true but misleading. Similarly, when a picture is offered for sale, the owner may take it to a world-famous expert who says that it is a worthless fake. There is nothing to prevent the advertiser from saying that, after consultation with the well-known expert, he is asking £100,000 for the picture.

Words are often misused in advertisements, but the motive

for their misuse is not necessarily an attempt to deceive. More often a word that has become a glamour-word is adopted without any clear idea of its meaning. A door-to-door salesman, who repeatedly described his product as 'guaranteed', was puzzled and rather offended when asked by whom it was guaranteed and against what. A similar uncertainty no doubt explains the description of a car polisher: 'Comes in genuine simulated alligator grain case for compact storage' (*Daily Telegraph*, 14 October 1970).

The advertiser likes to appeal to human cupidity. Reduction in price for quantities is a generally accepted commercial principle, which the advertiser uses to persuade customers to buy larger packets of the goods offered. So well known is this principle that a single word is enough to suggest to the customer that he will be given this reduction. That is why so many goods are now offered in the 'large economy size'. The name of the product can be a great help, or hindrance, to the advertiser. Many products today are sold all over the world and it is therefore necessary to choose a name that is easy to pronounce in many different languages. Judged by this test, *Kodak* and *Nylon* are good names; *Chiswick* is not.

Advertisers are sometimes ready to indulge in self-mockery, and readers who are unmoved by conventional approaches may fall victims to more sophisticated appeals like that in the dialogue: 'Do you read the — advertisements?', 'Yes, but I go on buying their product just the same.'

The words of an advertisement need to be chosen with care if a ludicrous effect is to be avoided. One shopkeeper put up a notice in his shop: 'No dissatisfied customer is ever allowed to leave these premises.' His aim was to emphasise his determination to please his customers, however exacting they might be, but his more imaginative customers had visions of a dungeon underneath the shop filled with dissatisfied customers who were not allowed to leave.

Personal advertisement columns offer hospitality to many linguistic eccentricities. The advertiser is sometimes conscious that the advertisement is costing a fairly large sum per line, as is the man who admits to being not only educated but also yg. and 'sks. 1/2 others to share a flt'. Considerations of cost give way to a love of euphemism in an advertisement which declares 'The fuller figure is no longer a problem'. The English love of animals assures a good response to the advertisements inserted, no doubt with some assistance, by pets seeking new homes. There is an appeal to the same love of animals in an advertisement which begins 'Dear little Jack Russell dog, $3\frac{1}{2}$, having lost devoted lady owner, seeks another.'

There are fashions in advertisement. At present the vogue-word in advertisements for secretaries seems to be 'top', a word which may owe its popularity to its use in *The Times* advertising campaign addressed to 'top people'. Five consecutive advertisements in one issue of a daily newspaper (*Daily Telegraph*, 15 January 1968) announce vacancies for 'top secretaries', a 'top flight secretary' and a 'top shorthand/typist'. Such frequency might lead one to think that 'top' is a technical term to describe a secretary in charge of an office, but another advertisement uses the word to describe the prospective employer: 'Top advertising agency needs young secretary.'

Until recently the impact of advertising on the average man was chiefly through the medium of the printed word. At fairs and in markets one could hear travelling salesmen extolling their wares in the manner of Dickens's Doctor Marigold, but these were not heard regularly by more than a small number of people. The coming of television commercials has greatly increased the use of the spoken word in advertising, and the results of the innovation are not always happy. The general standard of television acting is high, but the minor actors and actresses who enact brief scenes in the commercials often give way to the temptation to overact in order to make their point in the very short space of time at their disposal. The chief results of this overacting are that changes of intonation are too sudden and facial expressions too predictable. There is often a 'feed' who has the task of expressing astonishment at the low price of the product or who registers instant conviction on being assured of its virtues. Speakers are liable to extol their product with emotion dripping from every syllable, inducing in their more sensitive listeners a feeling of discomfort similar to that caused by the drawing-room performances of a child who has been praised for reciting with deep feeling. Affectation in pronunciation is not uncommon. In words like *path* the long back vowel, as heard in the South, is felt to be more respectable than the short vowel heard in the North, and consequently in television commercials *lather* is pronounced with an over-long vowel even though this is not the pronunciation that comes naturally to most of the viewers.

The term 'journalese', to describe the variety of language used in newspapers, is generally used disparagingly. There is nothing surprising in this. There is plenty of good writing to be found in newspapers, but this does not differ in essentials from other kinds of good writing; the features of newspaper English that are most noticeable are its faults, and it is to these that the term 'journalese' is generally applied. Journalists learn the danger of jumping to conclusions, and on occasion they show a cautious approach that many scholars might emulate. One reporter was shocked by the wording of a report that a man had gassed himself. When asked what was wrong with it, he replied: 'All that you know is that he was found dead in a gas-filled room.'

The chief characteristics, good and bad, of newspaper English arise from the fact that it is both written and read by people who are in a hurry. The good result of this requirement is that it must be clear and simple, with no involved sentences. Not all newspaper writing is alike. A leading article in *The Times*, dealing with a complicated subject, demands more complicated language than a short news paragraph. Mr Richard Usborne says that in the novels of P. G. Wodehouse Jeeves speaks 'copperplate *Times* Augustan' while Bertie Wooster speaks '*Sporting Life* vernacular'. He quotes in illustration:

> 'The scheme I would suggest cannot fail of success, but it has what may seem to you a drawback, sir, in that it requires a certain financial outlay.'
> 'He means,' I translated to Corky, 'that he has got a pippin of an idea but it's going to cost a bit.'[1]

The language of *The Times* is distinctive but far removed from what is generally thought of as journalese. It is usually formal, precise and pompous. Mrs Linda Berman[2] makes a

---

[1] Richard Usborne, *Wodehouse at Work* (Herbert Jenkins, 1961) p. 191.
[2] In an article to be published in the *Journal of the Lancashire Dialect Society*, XXII (1973).

good point in comparing the treatment of the men walking on the moon in *The Times* and the *Daily Mirror*. The former adopts NASA jargon and speaks of 'their period of extra-vehicular activity'; the latter says 'Ssh! It's bedtime for the moonmen! – the American astronauts were asleep on the moon last night'. American daily and weekly newspapers show similar variety. The theatrical newspaper *Variety* makes use of slang to an extent that makes it almost unintelligible to the uninitiated, while *Time* has developed a number of linguistic tricks, such as the use of blend-words like *vaudevilification* and the use of long and unusual nouns as verbs, giving preterites like *outnostalgiaed*.[1]

Journalese flourishes both in national newspapers with large circulations and in small local newspapers. It is as likely to occur in the correspondence columns as in the parts of the newspaper written by journalists, and thus it is reasonable to regard it as a register and not simply the occupational dialect of journalists. Anyone who is used to writing knows that, when writing in a hurry, one uses words that are too long; it is only on revision that a writer realises that his ideas can be expressed more simply. A letter in a provincial weekly contained the query 'As to the much talked-of Public Hall, will it ever be an actualisation?' The most noticeable features of journalese, which are, of course, not confined to that kind of writing, are excessive use of clichés, fondness for short paragraphs, inversion of normal word-order, fondness for irrelevant detail, sometimes expressed by the piling-up of adjectives and adjectival phrases, and occasional bad grammar.

Clichés abound in journalese because so much of the subject-matter of newspapers is repetitive material in which the journalist takes little interest. He has described similar events a hundred times before, and he therefore uses the phrases he has used a hundred times before, without realising how threadbare they have become. Sir Linton Andrews suggests that it is a good rule for young journalists that if a noun and an adjective seem to go inevitably together they deserve to be looked at askance; he instances *hasty retreat, sorry plight, canny Scot, gracious chatelaine*.[2] He goes on to complain of lovers of

[1] Berman, ibid.
[2] Sir Linton Andrews, *Problems of an Editor* (O.U.P., 1962) p. 85.

clichés who call attention to their own offence by putting the cliché within quotation marks. If a journalist puts idioms like 'a shot in the dark' and 'saving up for a rainy day' within quotation marks, one has to ask from what source are they quoted. They are drawn from the common stock of phrases which are available to everyone but which have been drawn upon too often.

Journalists are conscious of the danger of using too many tired phrases, but the attempt to avoid them by writing brightly is not free from dangers. A reporter, wishing to say that there would be five new players at a football match, produced the following opening sentence in a sports report: 'How many new faces will toe the line at Dens Park today? Echo answers five.'[1] Reporters become skilful at squeezing the last drop of emotion out of a commonplace situation by the use of words with emotive associations. If a man on trial wears spectacles, he is 'a bespectacled figure'; if a man tells a reporter to go away, he is described as 'tight-lipped', and if the reporter is annoyed at his refusal, there may be a headline 'Mounting anger at silence'.

The fondness for short paragraphs is a reaction against the nineteenth-century practice of presenting the reader with solid blocks of type which cunningly concealed the news from all but the most pertinacious reader. The other extreme of excessively short paragraphs had come into use already in the popular fiction of the nineteenth century, where it is possible to find a succession of paragraphs each consisting of a single short sentence. It has been suggested that one reason for the use of such short paragraphs was that the authors were paid by the line, and they therefore had every inducement to make a little go a long way, but we need seek no further for a motive than the writer's desire to arouse and keep his readers' interest. The following extract from a nineteenth-century novelette, *The Young Apprentice*, illustrates this style of writing:

> She could see every now and then glimpses of the road and the solitary windmill, whose phantom-like sails moved slowly some quarter of a mile away.
> This was all.
> No human being seemed here.

[1] Ibid., p. 72.

Not even a wild animal disturbed the stillness by leaping from its lair.

Yet presently, as I have said, footsteps seemed following her.

She stopped and listened.

All was still.

Then again she advanced.

The steps went on once more.

She became alarmed.

Should she go back?

Or should she hide herself?[1]

Writing of this kind is based on the assumption that readers are too impatient to read long paragraphs. Such a practice is reasonable if the thought is jerky, but it can make the reader's task harder if two sentences dealing with the same theme are split up into two separate paragraphs. Similarly, in the desire to avoid long unbroken paragraphs, subheadings are used, but these often interrupt the continuity of the thought.

The chief cause of inversion is the journalist's desire to put words that are likely to catch the reader's attention as near to the beginning of the sentence as possible. The word 'kitten' ranks high among such words, but a reporter paid a high price in order to give the word a prominent position:

A kitten was given priority when she took her eight-year-old son for an X-ray examination at Alder Hey Children's Hospital, Liverpool, Mrs Enid Parkes, 24, of Sunbeam Road, Liverpool, said last night.

Daily Telegraph, 1 February 1968

It is not until we reach the end of the sentence that we find out the real antecedent of 'her' in the first line.

Inversion, together with a fondness for combining odd bits of information into a single sentence, can produce some very clumsy sentences. The following sentence is part of the caption under an illustration in a newspaper:

Watching the contents of their home, including an 18th century grandfather clock, disappear yesterday into a container

[1] Quoted from E. S. Turner, *Boys will be Boys* (Michael Joseph, 1948) p. 34.

bound for Australia were Mr and Mrs Paul Lewis of Belmont, Surrey, and their children. Left to Right, Catherine, 9, Matthew, 2, Paul, 6, Anthony, 7, and Joanne, 5.

Daily Telegraph, 7 February 1969

An article, definite or indefinite, or the name of a nonentity does not arouse the reader's interest. It is a tradition of the popular press that 'Newsagent John Smith . . .' is a more arresting opening than 'Mr John Smith, a newsagent . . .'. In a book such openings are less necessary because a reader is less likely to leave a novel unread than a newspaper paragraph, though even a novelist, with the library public in mind, would be wise to make his first paragraph interesting, whatever happens afterwards.

Journalists often have to be vague because they are not free to specify the exact source of their information or because they have very little real news with which to fill up the space that the importance of their subject is deemed to demand. Readers thus become familiar with phrases like 'a spokesman' or 'usually well-informed sources in Paris'. A spokesman ought to mean somebody who can speak with authority on behalf of somebody else or of some body of people. The use of the word is always unsatisfactory, because the careful reader wants to know who the speaker is, so that he can judge with what authority he speaks. The word is used in journalese to mean 'some unnamed person who was willing to answer our reporter's questions'.

Perhaps by reaction from the vagueness that is sometimes imposed upon them, journalists often seem fond of quite irrelevant detail, such as the ages of minor participants in an incident or the tonnages of large steamships. It is reasonable to suppose that journalists know their own business and that such details are given because readers have made it clear that they want them. These bits of information can be given in separate sentences, but they are quite often incorporated into a single sentence by the free use of adjectives and adjectival phrases. This heavy qualification of the subject of a sentence gives a rhythm which is not usual in an English sentence. In English such heavy qualification generally follows the main verb and, to get the verb in as early as possible, journalese often uses inversion: 'Said 50-year old ex-army captain . . .' The following is a good example of the piling-up of adjectival phrases, one within the other like a set of Chinese boxes:

> Lord Justice Harman, with his wife and other members of his family, including grandchildren, sitting in court, then quoted from the Latin . . .
>
> *Daily Telegraph*, 6 June 1970

One reason for bad grammar in newspapers is that several people have had a hand in the production of a paragraph, all of them in a hurry. A corrector, glancing through a paragraph, may see 'three hitch-hikers was told' and he has no hesitation in correcting *was* to *were*. If he had had time to read the whole sentence, he would have found that it read 'The story of an accident to three hitch-hikers was told yesterday', and his correction has made nonsense of a perfectly grammatical, though undistinguished, sentence. Frequent proof-reading does much to reduce the number of mistakes in spelling, but some mistakes remain. A television critic wrote of an interviewer that his manner was 'perfectly judged between the differential and the patronising'. This comment is rather puzzling at first, but a moment's thought is enough to suggest to the reader that *differential* is a misspelling for *deferential*. This is the most dangerous type of spelling mistake. No great harm is done if the printer puts in *hubsand* for *husband*, but if his misspelling is another word, the hurried reader is in danger of not recognising that a mistake has been made.

Even in a single issue of a newspaper the language is not homogeneous. There are certain parts, such as sports and City pages, which can be almost meaningless to the uninitiated because of the special languages used. Regular readers understand the allusions and those who do not generally leave those pages alone. It is not merely a matter of technical terms, such as *bulls*, *bears* and *stags*, but of the idiomatic use of words and phrases whose meaning the reader thinks he knows. A single page of the *Daily Telegraph* (31 July 1967) speaks of a stock which 'went firmly ex-growth the same year' and speculates whether anyone ever does 'buy the index'. The writer may make the difficulty worse by literary allusion. Probably most English readers, even if they have not read *Through the Looking-*

Glass, will understand the allusion when a stock is described as 'a prime example of a jam tomorrow stock', but if a foreigner fails to understand it, a dictionary will not help him. The use of the word *jam* in the slang sense 'easy task' occurs in another passage which would cause trouble to a reader whose study of the English language had followed conventional lines:

> Most efficient plantations can make fair profits from an 18d. a lb. rubber price. Over that it becomes jam.
>
> *Daily Telegraph, 22 July 1969*

This is of the same kind as the gushing comment of the woman who was in raptures at the sight of some day-old chicks: 'Just look at these darling chickens. Aren't they ducks?'

The gossip columnist has his own type of sprightly badinage. Perhaps from fear of libel actions, he will avoid mentioning names of persons or places, while dropping enough hints to make it clear to his readers who is the person referred to. There is in gossip columns something of the effusive knowingness of a weak-minded aunt teasing her nephews and nieces by phrases like 'not a hundred miles from Westminster'.

Elegant variation is most common in sports journalism. There is a certain monotony about the events described which the journalist is tempted to disguise by finding new synonyms for such words as football ('the leather'), cricket-bat ('the willow') and goal-posts ('the uprights'). The sports page can be difficult reading for the casual reader. Here is an extract from an account of a football match:

> Knowles scored Wolves' fourth goal with the kind of audacity that made him famous. From a Wagstaff throw on the left Dougan chipped a pass in the direction of the Newcastle penalty spot. Knowles, with his back to the goal, volleyed straight over his left shoulder and inside the far post.

C. E. Montague's *A Hind Let Loose* (1910) is a satirical novel describing the activities of a very versatile Irish journalist. It is necessary to make allowance for the large element of burlesque in the specimens of the journalist's work that are quoted, but it is possible to find parallels to them in provincial newspapers. Strong language in leading articles is less common today than it used to be, and we have to turn to the *Eatanswill Gazette* for parallels to 'a compost of maudlin sentiment and gabbling abuse' or 'pragmatical pedants complicated with a touch of poltroon' (chap. 6). Vague criticism with little meaning is satirised in a passage which begins as a piece of music criticism but is used without change as a criticism of an exhibition of paintings. The first paragraph of the following extract is a specimen of the music criticism that is thus adapted; the second paragraph consists of the journalist's comments as he reads it through:

> 'The show as a whole is certainly some degrees richer than such shows often are in the elements of passion and sheer primal force, though cases will occur to every one in which these qualities verge dangerously on sentimentalism and melodrama. Possibly it also includes fewer of those obvious arrangements of checks and balances which may engage and satisfy the intellect, but leave the heart cold.'
> He paused for an instant, musing, 'You see, what it wants now is a technical tag. Turned on to pics, the best concert notice you'll find in the world is just the least taste general.' He sighed, 'Fact is – what you need, unless you're a real art critic, is seein' th'actual show.'
>
> Penguin ed., chap. 5

Another satirical novel dealing with journalism is Evelyn Waugh's *Scoop* (1933). This gives examples of the very distinctive variety of English used in press cablegrams to keep the number of words down to a minimum. Here too we have to remember that the author's aim is humour rather than authenticity. An inexperienced journalist sends a cable:

THEY HAVE GIVEN US PERMISSION TO GO TO LAKU AND EVERYONE IS GOING BUT THERE IS NO SUCH PLACE AM I TO GO TOO SORRY TO BE A BORE BOOT.

His more experienced colleague writes:

PERMISSION GRANTED LAKUWARD.

The reply sent to the inexperienced journalist is a good example of the condensed style:

UNPROCEED LAKUWARD STOP AGENCIES COVERING
PATRIOTIC FRONT STOP REMAIN CONTACTING CUMREDS
STOP NEWS EXYOU UNRECEIVED STOP DAILY HARD
NEWS ESSENTIALLEST STOP REMEMBER RATES SERVICE
CABLES ONE ETSIX PER WORD BEAST.

Penguin ed., bk II, chap. 6

Newspaper headlines use a language of their own, sometimes called block language, which influences other varieties of language. The most obvious need of newspaper headlines is compression in very little space, and short words are therefore preferred. Short words that are much used in headlines include *bid* (attempt), *trek* (journey), *ban* (to forbid), *rap* (to rebuke), *probe* (investigation), *pact* (treaty), and *reds* to describe anyone whose politics are left of those of the newspaper in which the headline appears. The verb *to wed* is now rather archaic in ordinary use, but it is much used in headlines, and it may well be that the revival of *Tories* as a name for members of the Conservative Party has been helped by the appeal that such a short word has for those who write headlines. Two linguistic conventions that have grown up in headlines are the use of the infinitive in place of the future ('Film Star to Wed') and the use of a comma when there is no room for the conjunction *and*, a practice parodied by a writer who created the sham headline 'Decline, Fall of the Roman Empire'. The use of the apostrophe to indicate the possessive case has almost ceased in headlines. Nouns in apposition are made to do the work of adjectives. This practice can lead to ambiguity. The headline 'Help the Aged Head' looks at first like an appeal for help on behalf of an elderly headmaster, but it simply describes the appointment of a new secretary-general of the charitable organisation called 'Help the Aged'. When headlines are set in block capitals, the reader is deprived of the help which initial capitals give in distinguishing between proper names and common nouns. It is not uncommon for four nouns in apposition to be piled up, as in 'Students Plan Grants Cuts Protest March'. Until the reader realises that 'plan' is a verb he may think that there are six nouns here, and some headlines are obscure because of the identity of form of many English nouns and verbs. One headline runs '£20,000 Range for Shooting Enthusiasts'. It makes a lot of difference to the enthusiasts to know whether *shooting* is a present participle or a noun. Other ambiguous headlines are 'Blind Man Expected to Leave Gaol' (Is *expected* a preterite or a past participle?), and '£1,900,000 Paid to Attack Victims' (Is *attack* a verb or a noun?). The ambiguity is usually only temporary; all but one of the theoretical possibilities can generally be ruled out as being contrary to common sense.

Initials are very freely used in headlines on the City page, to describe companies with cumbersome names. Some companies, such as Imperial Chemical Industries, are better known by their initials than by their full names. Others present some difficulty to the uninitiated. A single page of the *Daily Telegraph* for 5 August 1970 contained headlines referring to *U.B.M.*, *M.E.P.C.*, *I.W.T.O.*, *I.L.I.* and *I.O.S.* All but the last of these were printed in full in the news paragraph which followed the headline, and it was possible to discover that they referred to *United Builders Merchants*, *Metropolitan Estate and Property Co.*, *International Wool Textile Organisation*, *International Life Insurance* and *Investors Overseas Services*. The same issue contained a report on the progress of *Bats* (The British American Tobacco Co.), and this illustrates a further development in the use of initials: if they form a group that can be pronounced as a word they are treated like one.

The editors of City pages are fond of punning on the names or activities of the firms whose affairs they describe. The Rank Organisation gets a headline 'Pulling Rank', while a firm of salt manufacturers receives the more complicated headline: 'Will this Salt Seller Regain its Savour?'

Book titles can be regarded as another variety of block language. The prolix title-pages of the seventeenth century are out of fashion and conciseness is now the chief aim. There are fashions in the choice of titles. Quotations are less common than they were a few decades ago. The dangers of fanciful titles are illustrated by the mistakes made by unpractised cataloguers. The cataloguer who recorded 'Shelley's *Prometheus* (unbound)' was perhaps insufficiently familiar with the masterpieces of English literature, but Ruskin must share some of the blame for a librarian's inclusion under Agriculture of his theological pamphlet *Notes on the Construction of Sheeepfolds*. In choosing titles for works of non-fiction, authors and publishers often seem shy of precision lest it should limit the appeal of the book.

The title may be vague or misleading, while the real subject of the book is indicated in a subtitle.

The contribution of science to the English vocabulary has been greater during the present century than ever before. People are no longer content to leave science to the scientist, but there are popular writers on science who have introduced technical terms like *gene, hormone, chromosome, meson* and *cyclotron* to a wider public. With the increasing part played by scientific inventions in our everyday life, some technical terms cease to be technical and become everyday words. It would, for example, be absurd to think of *television* as a technical term. Some scientific terms, such as *transistor* and *antibiotic*, have become everyday words without their exact meaning being generally understood. Names of diseases pass into the everyday language and we sometimes forget how recent they are. *Appendicitis* did not find a place in the first volume of the *New English Dictionary* (1888) and had to wait for its inclusion until the publication of the Supplement in 1933. The new terms may be phrases made up of familiar words and they may owe their vogue to fashions in diagnosis; for example, *slipped disks* were until recently called by other names.

It has been said that it is a disadvantage of forming our new scientific vocabulary from classical roots that the meaning of such words is not immediately obvious, but this is not necessarily a disadvantage. As scientific knowledge advances, scientific terms outgrow their etymologies. The derivation of *electricity* from the Greek *elektron* (amber) now has little relevance, that of *oxygen* from French *oxygène* (acidifying principle) became inaccurate when it was found that oxygen was not the essential principle in the formation of acids, and that of *atom* from Greek *atomos* (indivisible) has became obsolete during the present century. There are advantages in the use of a completely new word, free from misleading associations with other words. One such word has passed into the everyday language. *Gas* was coined by van Helmont in the seventeenth century, and the only sign of its late introduction into the English language is that it has a short vowel, whereas in older words, such as *class* and *mask*, the *a* has been lengthened before the voiceless fricative consonant. For the most part scientific terms are not completely new; they have associations with other scientific terms containing the same roots, and the use of Greek and Latin roots has the advantage that these are internationally understood. It is possible for a man who has never consciously studied Greek to acquire a fair knowledge of Greek words and affixes from their use in English scientific terms.

Scientific terms are often long. Length does not necessarily add to their difficulty; what makes a word difficult is lack of associations. A long scientific word is made up of familiar elements which compress into one word facts that might have been expressed in several sentences. A long scientific word has two advantages: to a scientist it is self-explanatory and to a layman it is completely mysterious. This is an advantage because the layman realises that the word is unfamiliar to him and is not misled by associations that a familiar word would have for him if adopted for scientific use. Unfamiliar scientific terms can enjoy a constancy of meaning that they would not have if linked to everyday words that are constantly changing their meaning. Nevertheless, a layman cannot always see the point of a scientist's preference for technical terms, as when a naturalist, replying to a radio interviewer's question about birds of prey, clearly felt happier when he had translated *birds of prey* into *avian predators*.

Names of sciences tend to end in *-ology* (Gk. *logos*, 'a discourse') or *-ics* (Gk. suffix *-ikos*, Latin *-icus*, 'pertaining to'). Among the most recent terms of this kind are *hydroponics* (1938) and *cybernetics* (1946). This is defined as a 'collective term for the efforts – which have arisen in connection with the development of program-controlled computers, sometimes called rather misleadingly "electronic brains" – to understand problems of various specialist scientific and technical fields, especially in biology and information technology, as special cases of the same range of problems (information processing, control).' The book from which this definition is taken[1] provides a good example of the speed with which new sciences develop their own special vocabulary. Within twenty years of the creation of a new science it has developed a technical vocabulary that needs a book of more than 200 pages to explain it. The same book

[1] *Encyclopaedia of Cybernetics*, translated from the German by G. Gilbertson (M.U.P., 1968).

provides an illustration of the international nature of scientific vocabulary. Each term defined is translated into German, French and Russian, and for many of the terms the equivalents in the four languages are virtually identical. It calls for no great linguistic skill to translate into English the German *Kybernetik* or the French *cybernétique*, and there are other groups, such as *creativity, Creativität, créativité*, and *intelligence, Intelligenz, intelligence*. It has to be admitted, however, that not all the examples are as easy as this.

Flowering plants have a wide variety of popular names, both beautiful and fanciful. These are of little use to the botanist and are sometimes confusing, since the same plant may have many different names, and many plants have no popular name at all. The accepted method of naming living creatures was established by Carl Linnaeus. This system gives every organism a name consisting of two or three Latin words. The first of these is the name of the genus; the second is the 'trivial' name; and the two together are the specific name. The third word, if there is one, indicates the sub-species. These names are universally used in their Latin forms and are not translated.

A few scientific terms, such as *nucleus, focus* and *thorax*, have been borrowed intact from Greek or Latin, but most scientific terms of classical origin have been constructed from borrowed elements. The reason for the practice is that the classical languages happen to be very well suited for word-formation.

The high prestige of science today has had linguistic consequences that are not always happy. One of these is the use of the technical language of science in non-scientific contexts. Words like *matrix, agoraphobia, metabolism, syndrome* and *entropy* and phrases like *psychological moment* and *inferiority complex* become glamour-words for the non-scientific public. The introduction of such technical terms is one of the ways in which the language is enriched, but various abuses are possible. The two chief abuses in the use of technical terms are their unnecessary use and their incorrect use. If they are used to express ideas that can be expressed just as well in non-technical language, they simply interpose one more obstacle between the speaker and his hearers. The glamorous appeal of such words leads to their use by people without enough scientific knowledge to understand their true meaning, and the result is that even those who know their scientific meaning hesitate to use them because they know that they are liable to be misunderstood.

The suffix *-ology* is used to describe the study of that to which it is attached. Another suffix of similar meaning is *-graphy*, and the existence of two suffixes makes it possible to draw somewhat arbitrary, but generally accepted, distinctions between different aspects of a subject. Thus *geography* and *geology* describe different ways of studying the earth, and *biography* and *biology* both describe the study of life in two different senses of that word. Lovers of long words are fond of using words ending in *-ology* as synonyms of the words from which they are derived. Thus *ideology* can be defined as 'the science of ideas, the study of the nature and origin of ideas', but when we are told, as we often are, that we live in a world of conflicting ideologies, the speaker often means no more than a world of conflicting ideas. Similarly, *anatomy* means the study of the body, but it is often used as a semi-facetious synonym for *body*, especially when the speaker feels that a euphemism is called for.

Technical terms are always liable to be debased when they are freely used. *Chronic* and *acute* are medical terms to describe two different kinds of illness. A *chronic* illness is one which is lingering or which tends to recur, and is contrasted with an *acute* illness, which comes sharply to a crisis. In popular use, however, both adjectives are used as mere intensives to describe a severe illness. An invalid who feels that he is not getting enough sympathy may use either adjective to call attention to the severity of his sufferings.

One linguistic development shows how quickly scientific inventions can become old-fashioned. In the nineteenth century, steamships and steam locomotives were highly regarded examples of man's conquest of nature. During the present century steam is being superseded and is regarded as old-fashioned. Sound radio is suffering the same fate as a result of the invention of television, and consequently we find some people distinguishing between sound radio and television by calling the former *steam radio*. One journalist, taken to task by a correspondent for using this phrase, replied that he had used the word *steam* in the ironic and not the pejorative sense and that, as a devotee of railways, he regarded *steam radio* as a term of praise (*Daily Telegraph*, 6 June 1970).

Religion has its special linguistic varieties, both spoken and written. A clergyman has to make himself heard in a large church and he therefore has to speak loudly, clearly and slowly while conducting a service, and he often carries these habits into his everyday life. In Anglican services intoning is a common practice. It became widespread in nineteenth-century England and was associated with the Oxford Movement. If Barchester was a typical diocese, the practice did not at first command many adherents. Anthony Trollope says of the clergymen of Barchester:

> The services were decently and demurely read in their parish churches, chanting was confined to the cathedral, and the science of intoning was unknown. One young man who had come direct from Oxford as a curate to Plumstead had, after the lapse of two or three Sundays, made a faint attempt, much to the bewilderment of the poorer part of the congregation. Dr Grantly had not been present on the occasion; but Mrs Grantly, who had her own opinion on the subject, immediately after the service expressed a hope that the young gentleman had not been taken ill, and offered to send him all kinds of condiments supposed to be good for a sore throat. After that there had been no more intoning at Plumstead Episcopi.
>
> *Barchester Towers* (1857) chap. 6

One of the signs by which the general public recognise a clergyman's profession is that his intonation is liable to show variations not demanded by the sense of what he is saying. When intonation and sense do correspond, clergymen sometimes use more extreme forms of intonation than the common man. One result of speaking slowly and clearly is that lightly stressed vowels are often pronounced as though they were fully stressed, and, when final, are sometimes lengthened and distorted, whereas most people reduce such vowels to the central vowel [ə]. Thus we find [fɔːtʃuːn] 'fortune', [litərətʃuaː] 'literature' and [ðɛaː] 'there'. Further features of clerical English are:

(1) A tendency to vary vowel-length by analogy with related words. Thus, the *ow* of *knowledge* is often pronounced [ou], on the analogy of *know*.

(2) A tendency to raise [æ] to [e], thus obscuring the difference between *man* and *men*.

(3) The use of clear [l] in all positions. French and Italian singing teachers have been blamed for this, since dark *l* is not found in those languages.

(4) The use of intrusive *r*, as in *lawr and order*.

(5) The use of the singular forms of the second personal pronoun in addressing God in prayer, with the consequential use of the archaic second-person singular verbal forms. This practice was well established until about the middle of the present century, but there is now an increasing tendency to replace *thou* by *you*.

(6) The use of archaic words such as *unto* (to), *morrow* (morning) or *Sabbath* (Sunday).

(7) The use of familiar words in an archaic or specially religious sense: *ever* (always), *me* (myself), *magnify* (praise), *through* (by the intercession of).

The Lord's Prayer is often recited aloud in chorus at speed, and then lightly stressed syllables are liable to disappear. Triphthongs are badly treated and so the Prayer often seems to begin 'Ah, father, chart in Heaven'. The concluding 'Amen' is pronounced variously (ɑːˈmen] and [eiˈmen]. The latter pronunciation has been said to be especially common among Roman Catholics, but it is often used by members of other denominations. It is sometimes said that words like *mass* and *Catholic* are pronounced with long stem-vowels by members of some religious denominations but with short vowels by others. There have been investigations on these lines but the results are inconclusive. Further inquiries with more rigorous sampling procedures might produce interesting results.

In vocabulary and syntax the chief characteristic of religious language is the fondness for archaism, which may be due in part to the prestige of the Authorised Version of the Bible and the Book of Common Prayer. The influence of religious language can be seen in the use of quite simple and everyday words. When an orator referred to an election result in which he took a keen interest he spoke of what had been achieved 'this day'. By using this phrase instead of the more colloquial 'today' he was obviously trying to emphasise the importance of the event, and no doubt one reason why he was able to do so is that the daily use of 'this day' in the Lord's Prayer gives it for most of us associations that remove it from triviality.

Archaism often causes children to misunderstand hymns. One child who had frequently sung 'There is a green hill far away, without a city wall', asked why a green hill should be expected to have a city wall; he was not familiar with the use of *without* in the sense 'outside'. Very young children are content to sing words without insisting that they should have any meaning. One child sang the hymn 'Jesus high in glory' some hundreds of times, thinking all the time that the first three words were 'Jesus iron glory'.

Evelyn Waugh's *Decline and Fall* (1928) gives an example of the use of hymns as a medium of conversation by the inmates of a prison, who rely on the warders' failure to listen to the middle of the verses:

> All over the chapel the men filled their chests for a burst of conversation:
>
> > 'O God, our help in ages past', sang Paul,
> > 'Where's Prendergast to-day?'
> > 'What, ain't you 'eard? e's been done in.'
> > 'And our eternal home.'
> >   Penguin ed., part III, chap. 3

A linguistic feature of some hymns is the failure of the tune to fit the words, which have to be sung in a way that is out of accord with natural speech-rhythm. It is, of course, inevitable that the intonation of hymns should differ from that of speech. It is the essence of singing that the pitch remains uniform on one note and then changes quickly to pass to another note; the intonation is changing in a series of steps, whereas in speech such level pitch is used only for special reasons, such as parenthesis. Other special features of hymn-singing can be avoided if the tune and words are carefully matched when the hymn is set to music. Such features include the undue lengthening of certain vowels and the stressing of unimportant words. Such unnatural stressing can be heard in the hymn 'Jesu, lover of my soul', where the usual tune demands that great prominence should be given to the word 'of'. The problems of the English hymn-writer are, however, slight compared with those of a

composer setting hymns to music in a language where the
intonation changes the meaning of words. Lloyd James reports
that the hymn 'Holy, Holy, Holy' sung in Mandarin Chinese
to its usual English tune, means 'Fresh Vegetables, Fresh
Vegetables, Fresh Vegetables'.[1]

[1] James, *The Broadcast Word*, p. 10.

5

Slang

SLANG is a variety of language which arouses the most diverse responses. Probably the earliest response which most of us can remember is one of disapproval: children are reproved for using words, picked up from their friends, which seem to them wonderfully expressive but which for some reason have little appeal for their parents. Later they may find the offending words used by the very people who have protested at their use, or they may find that in certain circumstances derision or hostility is aroused by the use of a standard English word in a group of people among whom slang is the normal medium of communication. A sixth-form schoolboy, visiting a Cambridge college for an interview, asked an undergraduate the way to the lavatory and received the haughty reply 'The bogs are over there'. There is no contradiction between these two points of view. Slang is a good example of a linguistic register in that its proper use depends chiefly on the occasion when it is used, though, like other registers, it can be regarded to some extent as a matter of idiolect and to some extent one of dialect, since certain groups, especially young people, are especially fond of slang. Particular professions, such as the Navy and the stage, have their own varieties of slang, which take on some of the features of occupational dialect.

Slang is not an easy term to define. *C.O.D.* (5th ed., 1964) gives two definitions. The first is: 'Words and phrases in common colloquial use, but generally considered in some or all of their senses to be outside of standard English.' This definition calls attention to two of the characteristics of slang: it is chiefly concerned with vocabulary and it is more at home in the spoken than the written language. The rest of the definition is open to the objection that it says what slang is not rather than what it is. At least two other varieties of speech are generally considered to be outside the standard language, namely dialect and vulgarisms, and it is necessary to find a definition of slang that will distinguish it from these. Slang differs from dialect in two of its characteristics: it is usually novel whereas dialect is usually deep-rooted in the past, and it is used deliberately by speakers who could express their ideas more simply, but who avoid the obvious, straightforward word for the sake of novelty or vividness. This same quality of deliberateness will serve to distinguish slang from vulgarisms. A man uses a vulgarism because he doesn't know any better; he uses slang from choice. The deliberate nature of slang may be illustrated by the use of *telly* for *television*. Originally a vulgarism, comparable with such curtailments as *chocs* for *chocolates* and *advert* for *advertisement*, it has now a wider currency as slang. When educated people speak of the *telly*, they generally do so with a slight smile that is the visual equivalent of quotation marks. Television has brought with it its own range of slang expressions. Those who find *telly* too formal will describe a television set as a *goggle-box* or *the one-eyed monster*, while a set that is out of order is said to be *on the blink*.

The second meaning of *slang* given by *C.O.D.* is 'words and phrases either entirely peculiar to or used in special senses by some class or profession.' This kind of slang is sometimes called cant, and it can best be regarded as an occupational dialect. The two terms *slang* and *cant* are often considered together because many words belong to both groups. One thing that they have in common is that they both tend to be regarded as substandard.

An essential characteristic of slang is its informality. A second, less essential, characteristic is that it is often highly idiomatic, and it is consequently dangerous to try to use slang when speaking a foreign language. Talking slang is like walking downstairs: if it comes naturally, nothing could be easier, but if the speaker has to think what he is doing and to watch every step, he is likely to meet with a mishap. The proper use of slang calls for considerable linguistic tact. By using slang a speaker is making advances towards his hearers, and he should be prepared to recognise signs that those advances are unwelcome and that his hearers would prefer a more formal relationship.

Slang sometimes consists of entirely new words of uncertain etymology like *stooge, twerp, scrounge* and *gallivant*. It may consist of derivatives of well-known words, like *mizzle* (to disappear), a back-formation from *misled*, or *brekker* for *breakfast*. Sometimes only one sense of a word is slang while the other senses belong to the conventional standard language. An example is the use of *it* in the sense of 'sex-appeal'. It is perhaps a result of the popularity of slang among students that a number of slang words have had a learned origin. *Nous* (good sense) is from the Greek, and *tandem*, the name of a bicycle made for two, is a pun on the Latin *tandem* (at length). Foreign phrases have given rise to English slang words, and some of these have passed into the standard language, like *hoax* (Latin *hocus pocus*), and *mob* (Latin *mobile vulgus*).

It is often difficult to decide whether a given idiom is slang or colloquial; phrases on the border-line include *you can't see the wood for the trees, to go at something tooth and nail, to kick your heels*. Time makes slang accepted, especially if a phrase is used by a famous writer, like *to cudgel one's brains*, used in Shakespeare only by vulgar characters. Proverbial phrases enter largely into everyday conversation, and some of these phrases are slang while others are standard English. There are often many different ways of expressing a single idea. The variety adds to the richness, but also to the difficulty of the language; the difficulty arises in choosing the right degree of informality to suit a particular occasion. Thus, to express disapproval of someone who makes a fuss about trifles, one could use a proverbial idiom and say 'Don't make mountains out of molehills' or a colloquialism and say 'Don't make such heavy weather of it'. Both of these protests belong to the range of standard English, but the user of slang can draw on other resources, which some would regard as more friendly but others as less so, and he might say 'All right, don't make a meal of it'. The dialect speaker has still further resources, and he can ask for 'not so many feetmark'. Similarly, to indicate that he has understood a point in an argument, a man might use standard English and say 'I take your point', or he might use a colloquialism 'I've got the message', or he could use slang 'All right, the penny's dropped'.

Some phrases which have a generally accepted standard

English meaning acquire a second meaning as slang. Thus, when silent films gave way to talking pictures, all cinemas were described as being *wired for sound*; the phrase is used as slang to describe anyone wearing a hearing-aid. The phrase *vital statistics* has long been used by actuaries to refer to statistics dealing with birth, marriage and death; it is widely used today to describe the bust, waist and hip measurements of shapely young women. The same sort of thing can happen with words as well as phrases. By giving one element of a compound word a special sense, it is possible to give an entirely new, and often jocular, meaning to the compound. Thus, *guinea-pig* comes to be used as an insulting term for a company director, and *semi-detached*, normally applied to houses, is used to describe a man living apart from his wife but not divorced.

One characteristic of slang which arises from the attribute of novelty is that slang words have a very short life in the language. Whereas the words which form the backbone of the language have for the most part had a life of more than a thousand years and still show no signs of failing vitality, it is unusual for slang words to remain in use for more than a few years, though some slang terms serve a useful purpose and so pass into the language. *Blurb* (a publisher's eulogy) was originally American slang but it may now be said to have passed into standard English. Slang words are invented by a few people for the pleasure of novelty and imitated by others who like to be in the fashion, and they undergo the fate of all fashions. Many of the slang words coined during the Second World War have passed out of use along with the events that called them into life. Users of slang delight in topical allusions. For example, shortly after the introduction of the National Health Service a man looking for his spectacles said: 'Where are my National 'Ealths?' On recognising the allusion the reader or the hearer experiences a little glow of satisfaction comparable with the self-congratulatory zest with which the members of a studio audience applaud loudly at any topical reference in a radio variety programme, to make it clear that they have understood the allusion.

Excessive use of a word in a slang sense may destroy the value of the word in legitimate use. In the early nineteenth century it was possible for a poet to describe a young lady as a blooming girl, or for a man to say that he had been wounded by a bloody spear, but no longer.

Slang is so popular that it is worth while to inquire why people use it. When those who use slang are asked why they do so, the most frequent replies are 'Habit' and 'Imitation'. Both these are quite important causes of the spread of slang words once they have come into existence, but they throw no light on the origin of slang, and they apply equally well to other kinds of language, not especially to slang. Indeed, slang is rather an attempt to avoid some of the evils of habit and imitation in the use of language. Once these motives come to play an important part in the transmission of words, they cease to be slang and become part of the standard language. A more valuable hint about the origin of slang words is provided by another popular reply: many American students said that they use slang for the sake of conciseness and emphasis. One reason why people use slang is that they want to add liveliness to what they are saying; they don't want to seem stilted or formal. Another motive is the desire for a greater sense of intimacy in the use of language: that is why slang is especially common among friends. Another motive is discontent with hackneyed words and phrases. Slang can be used to bring an air of friendly informality to a situation. The B.B.C. is sometimes accused of being stodgy, and it was no doubt the desire to get away from this image that caused one of their announcers, introducing a magazine programme, to apologise for being late by saying breezily that he had 'got stuck in the loo', and on another occasion to say 'You must have thought we'd gone potty. We played the wrong tapes.' Young people are notoriously fond of refusing to accept the standards of their elders; in using slang they are carrying this refusal into the realm of language. Sudden excitement or periods of artificial life when our habits are forcibly changed generally lead to an increase in the use of slang. That is why war generally leads to the introduction of many new slang words.

There are many minor reasons why people use slang, and each of these reasons accounts for one group of slang words. One such motive is the love of euphemism, the desire to gloss over unpleasant things, such as death and drunkenness. Shakespeare uses euphemisms quite often when he refers to death; Macbeth's *taking off* has its parallel in the slang *bumping off*.

Slang can be used, like dialect, to soften the asperity of a rebuke, provided that it is used with tact on an appropriate occasion. A company chairman cannot call a meeting to order by asking for 'bags of 'ush', but that was the phrase used with success by a North Country chairman of a less formal meeting.

Another reason why some people use slang is that it is capable of becoming a secret language. It is often useful to have some means of conveying information without allowing other people to understand what you are saying. Such secret language flourishes among many groups of people today, for example in the underworld and in many schools.

There are other reasons for using slang which appeal to more sophisticated and educated people. Among such motives has been mentioned a deliberate desire to enrich the language or to lend an air of solidity or reality to an abstract discussion. Those who use slang would be quick to disclaim any such motives, which would seem to them absurdly pompous, but, if enrichment of the language is not as a rule a motive for the use of slang, it is sometimes a result. The user of slang is constantly experimenting, and it is only by a willingness to experiment that it is possible to give to a language the amazing complexity and power to express subtle shades of meaning that present-day English has acquired. The effect of slang on a language is not generally very lasting. Slang words as a rule express ideas which can be expressed equally well by the ordinary language, so there is little incentive to allow them to become permanent. Terms of abuse tend to be borrowed freely from slang. Words describing crime naturally tend to be borrowed from thieves' slang, and so we have *rogue, bully, to filch* and *to foist*.

The effect of slang on a language is neither wholly good nor wholly bad. It introduces new meanings but it also tends to remove delicate shades of meaning in existing words and leads to over-emphasis and a straining after effect. It is the fate of most well-known slang expressions to strike the popular fancy and to be over-used until they become more threadbare than the words that they were intended to replace. Slang words tend to be vogue-words and their excessive use leads to a reaction against them. Few forms of speech create such an unfavourable impression as out-of-date slang. On the other hand, slang is interesting because, when it is new, it is the aspect of language that is most intensely alive, and in it we can watch linguistic processes at work without the restrictions which the standard language imposes on them. There is no essential difference between the processes of slang and those of standard speech.

Slang includes many monosyllabic words that express everyday ideas concisely. Such words are *nosh* (meal) borrowed from Yiddish, and *kip* (sleep). Some of the longer slang words seem to have been coined because someone thought the sounds pleasing or appropriate. Thus in nineteenth-century slang we have *ferricadouzer* (a good thrashing), *absquatulate* (to go away) and *catawamptious* (eager). Vague associations with other words have probably played a part in the creation of slang words, as they have with some words in standard English. Some of the longer slang words are playful extensions of common English words, and these are sometimes nonce-words or words with a very short life. Even if the word occurred only once, we should be able to guess the meaning of the man who expressed a fear that, if his employer heard about his behaviour, he might be dejobulated. Most slang, however, does not result from the coining of new words but from giving new senses to old words or from combining quite simple and everyday words into new idiomatic phrases. Phrases are often slang when the constituent words are not. Examples are: *to step on the gas, to miss the boat, dead between the ears, fed up, an also-ran, a pain in the neck, a nasty bit of work, I'm not with you, with it. This is where we came in* is taken over from the language of the cinema to be used as a protest when conversation or wrangling is becoming repetitive. A phrase may be deliberately ungrammatical: hardly any of those who speak cheerfully of reading *whodunits* would ever ask *Who done it?* in any other context. The word is a loan from substandard English. Substandard phrases like 'the lady what does for us' and 'Let 'em gnash 'em as 'as 'em' can be heard from the delicately nurtured as quotations from the real or supposed dialect of members of a different social class.

Angry letters written to newspapers sometimes give the impression that all slang is American. This assumption is incorrect. Slang can come into existence at any time in any language, though some societies are more hospitable to it than others. The reason why many Englishmen tend to equate slang and American English is that American slang is often much more picturesque and striking than British, and it has therefore been freely introduced into England. British slang tends to include words of uncertain etymology, like *bally* and *swank*, and perversions of common words, like *brekker* for *breakfast*. American slang makes greater use of picturesque imagery and produces words like *skyscraper*, *bell-hop* and *lounge-lizard*.

One kind of slang that enjoys wide currency today and which enjoyed an even wider vogue during the nineteenth century is the catch-phrase, which often had its origin in some forgotten popular song or in some jocular greeting. Many of these phrases are used as part of the ritual of convivial drinking. Blameless young men say to one another *Success to crime!* or *Mud in your eye!* and *Cheers!* is still widely used. When saying farewell, they are liable to say *Don't do anything I wouldn't do, Look after yourself* or *Be seeing you*. With constant use catch-phrases can become virtually meaningless. *How's your poor feet?* is a rather old-fashioned form of jocular greeting; the suggestion that it had its origin during the Exhibition of 1851 carries conviction.

The debt of standard languages to slang may be greater than we realise, since we cannot always tell which words, now quite formal and respectable, were once regarded as slang. The French and Italian words for 'head', *tête* and *testa*, are often quoted as examples of common words which had their origin in slang, since they go back to the Latin slang use of *testa* (pot) replacing the more respectable *caput*. English words which were once slang include *clumsy, humbug, bogus, strenuous, mob* and the phrase *at fault*, originally used of hounds that have lost the scent. Words that occur frequently in literature can sometimes be identified as slang if they are used only by low-life characters or on informal occasions. For example, in the drinking scenes in *Twelfth Night* we find words like *clay-brained* and *knotty-pated* both meaning 'stupid', *gorbellied* (fat), *testril* (sixpence), *bawcock* (good fellow; cf. French *beau coq*), *kickshaws* (trifles; cf. French *quelquechose*), and the phrase *Sneck up* (Be off). All of these give the impression of being slang.

In sixteenth-century England the slang of the underworld is not only used by pamphleteers but is discussed and explained.

E

Robert Greene wrote a series of pamphlets, generally known as
Cony-Catching Pamphlets, to expose the exploits of Elizabethan
confidence tricksters, and in *A Notable Discovery of Coosnage*
(1591) he included glossaries of their secret vocabulary. He
listed eight categories of villainy, each with its own special
terms. These are:

1	High law	robbing by the highway side.
2	Sacking law	lecherie.
3	Cheting law	play at false dice.
4	Cros-biting law	cosenage by whores.
5	Conycatching law	cosenage by cards.
6	Versing law	cosenage by false gold.
7	Figging law	cutting of purses, & picking of pockets.
8	Barnards law	a drunken cosenage by cards.

Detailed vocabularies are given for all the eight categories
except one, but when he comes to 'Cheting law' Greene is
mysteriously reticent, no doubt to whet the reader's curiosity:

> Pardon me Gentlemen for although no man could better
> then my self discouer this lawe and his tearmes, and the
> name of their Cheats, Barddice, Flats, Forgers, Langrets,
> Gourds, Demies, and many other, with their nature, &
> the crosses and contraries to them vpon aduantage, yet for
> some speciall reasons, herein I will be silent.[1]

The slang of fashionable society during the early eighteenth
century is well portrayed in Swift's *Polite Conversations*, where
we find such jests as 'Faith, I'm for Bedfordshire', a phrase
meaning 'I'm going to bed', later used by Parson Woodforde
and others. In the nineteenth century the novels of Dickens
provide many examples of the use of slang. In *Oliver Twist*
the language of the underworld still flourishes, and the Game
Chicken in *Dombey and Son* is most eloquent when using the
slang of prize-fighters. The letters and reported conversations
of eminent Victorians contain a good deal of slang. Rossetti
speaks of *tin* for 'money' and Turner is reported to have said

[1] Robert Greene, *A Notable Discovery of Coosnage 1591, The Second Part of
Cony-Catching 1592*, ed. G. B. Harrison, Bodley Head Quartos (John Lane,
1923) pp. 37–8.

'Yes, Mr Ruskin, art is a rum go'. There is a certain pathos in the remark of the Duke of Wellington when rioters broke the windows of his house on the anniversary of the Battle of Waterloo: 'Rum day to choose.' In the present century the literary possibilities of the use of slang have been well illustrated in both England and America. Galsworthy's *The White Monkey* (1924) shows the popularity of slang in the England of the 1920s. That novel contains the following synonyms for 'rubbish, nonsense': *tosh, tripe, pop* (short for *poppycock*), *gup, pulp, bilge, drivel* and *guff*.[1] The dangers of the excessive use of slang by a novelist are illustrated in the short stories of the American O. Henry. Once very popular, some of them are now almost unreadable because the slang with which they abound is virtually meaningless to a reader of today.

Because slang changes so quickly, it is possible to study its history during what is, in terms of the history of a language, a short period. A Victorian youth would express emphatic agreement by saying *I believe you*; today he would say *You can say that again*. The exact meaning of Victorian slang phrases like *up to snuff* is not always obvious and the etymology may be even more obscure. Sometimes a slang routine may involve more than one participant. At the beginning of the twentieth century roars of laughter were provoked by an exchange of the type:

'What's the matter with James?'
'He's all right.'
'Who is?'
Chorus, in which everyone present was expected to join: 'James!'

One special kind of slang used originally by showmen and strolling players and later by cheapjacks is parlyaree.[2] Most of the words are of Italian origin but a few are from Romany

[1] Eric Partridge, *Slang To-day and Yesterday* (Routledge, 1935) p. 125.
[2] The best short account of parlyaree is by Eric Partridge, *Here, There and Everywhere* (Hamish Hamilton, 1950) pp. 116–25, and most of the examples quoted here are from that source. Some examples of parlyaree words are included in Wilfred Granville, *A Dictionary of Theatrical Terms*, The Language Library (André Deutsch, 1952).

languages. The name is derived from the Italian verb *parlare*, possibly influenced by such a part of the verb as *parliamo*. The close resemblance to Italian can be seen by comparing the parlyaree numerals *una, dooe, tray, quater, chinker, sa, setter, otter, nobber, dacha* with Italian *una* (fem.), *due, tre, quattro, cinque, sei, sette, otto, nove, dieci*. A theatrical term is *nanty dinarly*, '(There is) no money'. *Medzer* (Italian *mezzo*, 'half') means 'halfpenny'; *medzers* or *metzes* means 'money' and *nanty metzes* therefore means 'penniless'. *Medza caroon* means 'half a crown'. Other coins are *ponte* (pound), *quartereen* (farthing), *salty* (penny) and *bianc* (shilling), from Italian *bianco* (white). A man is an *omee* (cf. Italian *uomo*) and a policeman is a *charpering omee*. A woman is a *donah* or a *pollone*, and children are called *chavies* or *chavvies*, a Romany word, and also *feeliers* (cf. Italian *figli*, 'sons'). A bed is a *letty* (Italian *letto*). Since parlyaree is spoken more often than written, spelling can disguise the origin of a word: *carser*, 'a house', is less obvious than its variant *casa*, from Italian *casa*. The word for food has many variant forms: *manjaree, monjaree, munjaree, numyare*, all from Italian *mangiare* (to eat), and the word for a drink is *bevvy* (cf. early Italian *bevere*, 'to drink'). Two adjectives that are much used are *bono* (good) and *catever* (bad), from Italian *bono* (early and dialectal) and *cattivo* respectively.

Rhyme plays a part in many slang expressions, especially in the exuberant expansions of simpler slang words, such as *super-duper* (excellent), *okey-doke* (all right). Rhyming slang is a special kind of substitution where rhyme provides the key to the meaning of the slang word: one word is replaced by another of quite different meaning that happens to rhyme with it. Examples are *dicky bird* (word), *no soap* (no hope), *half-inch* (pinch, i.e. steal), *tea-leaf* (thief), *almond rocks* (socks), *apples and pears* (stairs), *a ball of chalk* (a walk), *turtle-doves* (gloves), *Mutt and Jeff* (deaf), *Rory O' More* (door), *Pat Malone* (alone), *Phil MacBee* (flea), *brass tacks* (facts). At a later stage of the development of this kind of slang the rhyming word is omitted, as in *tit for* (*tat*) (hat), *Oxford* (*scholar*) (dollar, or its equivalent in another currency), *elephant's* (*trunk*) (drunk), *loaf* (*of bread*) (head), *China* (*plate*) (mate). One kind of slang which can easily become tiresome or mechanical is back slang, where a word is spelt backwards with the insertion of vowels to avoid unpronounceable consonant groups: *kacab genals* (back slang), *tekram* (market). Back slang is often only approximate; for example, *kew* means 'week' and *nosper* 'person'. Gibberish is a disguised language formed by inserting a consonant at the end of each syllable: *Howg dog youg dog?* means 'How do you do?' It was once popular among children but is not much used today.

Slang is remarkable for its wealth of synonyms, a natural result of the constant quest for novelty. The fields which are richest in synonyms reflect the interests of the speakers. Policemen enter a good deal into the lives of speakers of slang and it is therefore natural that there should be many slang synonyms for a policeman. They illustrate the many different ways in which slang words come into use. *Copper* has nothing to do with the metal; a copper is one who cops or catches. *Flatty* is an unsympathetic allusion to the effect on the feet of a job which at one time involved a lot of standing. *Slop* is back slang, with the consonants of *police* in reverse order. *Bobby* is a survival of a topical allusion; it is from the Christian name of Sir Robert Peel, the founder of the police force. More recent synonyms are *pig* and *fuzz*.

The ideas most productive of slang synonyms are death, sex, physical violence and drunkenness. This range of subjects is in part a reflection of the interests of those who use slang and in part a result of the search for euphemism. The large number of synonyms for drunkenness is no doubt due to exuberance as much as to euphemism. As so often when synonyms are in question in the standard language, we often find that words of similar meaning are not exact synonyms. A man might admit to being squiffy but indignantly deny that he was blotto. It is not only unpleasant ideas that call forth large numbers of synonyms. A character in a novel by P. G. Wodehouse provides many translations of a slang phrase, none of them standard English:

> Bream Mortimer looked somewhat apprehensive.
> 'You won't tell him that I was the one who spilled the beans?'
> 'I beg your pardon?'
> 'You won't wise him up that I threw a spanner into the machinery?'

'I do not understand you.'

'You won't tell him that I crabbed his act . . . gave the thing away . . . gummed the game?'

'I shall not mention your chivalrous intervention.'[1]

The numerous synonyms for money include *brass, lolly, tin, dough, mazuma, moolah, dash, splosh, bees and honey,* and, recently, *bread.* A pound is a *quid,* a *smacker* or a *nicker;* ten shillings is *half a nicker* or *half a bar;* five shillings is a *dollar;* a shilling is a *bob,* a *diener* or a *thumber;* sixpence is a *tanner,* a *kick* or a *sprat;* threepence is a *bit* or a *tiddler.* Copper coins are *mouldies.* A penny is a *clod* or a *dee* (preceded by a numeral). A halfpenny is a *meg* or a *rusty meg.* Like their standard English equivalents these slang terms remain in use after the coins that they describe have been replaced by other coins.

Parts of the body are often described by slang terms. 'Head' is *nob, nut, loaf, bones, block* or *dome;* 'face' is *mug, dial* or *phiz;* 'nose' is *conk, beak, snitch, snout, snozzle* or *boko;* 'mouth' is *gob;* 'ears' are *flaps* or *lugs;* 'hands' are *mitts* or *dukes.*

Slang words expressing vague approval are commonly used, especially by children. *Topping* and *ripping* are now dated. So too are the more recent *wizard, super* and *super-duper.* Other words frequently used are *fabulous, lush, snazzy, groovy, swell* and *supersonic.* The approval need not be vague. A *whizz-kid* is a man who achieves success by his energy and progressive ideas, while the *jet-set* is a social group whose members can afford to spend most of their time in pleasure resorts, often in remote places. Words expressing dislike are even more numerous. They include *chronic, daft, lousy, grotty, mouldy, putrid, rotten, stinking* and *flipping awful.* Some words express both praise and blame: *kinky* means 'eccentric', and it is used in both praise and dispraise and in a mixture of the two to describe some aberration generally thought to be wrong, although it is often clear that the speaker does not share that view. Food is *bait, chuck, grub, grubber, munchie, tuck, tucker* or *scranner.*[2] There are many ways of expressing resentment at interference: *Belt up, Drop dead, Get knotted, Get stuffed* or *Go and take a long walk on a short pier.*

[1] *The Girl on the Boat* (Herbert Jenkins, 1922) chap 1.
[2] Opie, *The Lore and Language of Schoolchildren,* p. 155.

The wealth of synonyms in slang does not cause much trouble because the context usually makes clear the meaning of any new expression, to say nothing of the knowing leer with which the user of slang makes it clear that he has discovered yet another way of saying that he was drunk. Foreigners may have rather more difficulty, because they are likely to have acquired their knowledge of English in the formal atmosphere of the class-room, where slang would be out of place. Some teachers of languages try to overcome this difficulty by teaching their pupils slang idioms, but there are dangers in this practice. Slang changes so quickly that it is likely to be out of date be-fore it reaches the classroom, and the effective use of slang demands a feeling for delicate shades of formality that cannot be expected from anyone who needs classroom instruction. To understand slang is much easier than to use it, and instruc-tion in the understanding of slang either by word of mouth or by the use of dictionaries can be useful. A manual has been published to help overseas doctors working in Great Britain to understand the language, mostly euphemistic and a good deal of it slang, that their patients are likely to use.[1] The author quotes a number of euphemisms for the verb 'to die'; they include *to be a goner, to conk out, to kick the bucket, to have had it, to peg out, to push up daisies, to turn it in* and *to turn one's toes up*. To describe drunkenness, degrees of comparison are necessary. Words meaning 'slightly drunk' include *fresh, lush, squiffy, tiddly* and *tight*; words meaning 'very drunk' include *soaked, sozzled* and *stoned*; a man who is confused with drink is *fuddled* or *woozy*. Phrases describing pregnancy include a large number that are 'not commonly used in polite society'. These include *to be in pig, to be in the pudding club, to be preggers, to be up the pole, to have a bun in the oven* and *to have a touch of the sun*. Not all the words and phrases are slang. To describe some-one who feels unwell there are slang words like *groggy, wobbly* and *wonky*, beside idiomatic colloquial phrases like *off colour, out of sorts, run down*, and phrases that could be described as vul-garisms rather than slang, such as the very common *to feel funny*. The stomach disorder that is likely to attack visitors to hot countries has a variety of slang names: *Gippy tummy*,

---

[1] Joy Parkinson, *A Manual of English for the Overseas Doctor* (E. & S. Livingstone, 1971).

Delhi belly, Rangoon runs, Tokyo trots and *Montezuma's revenge*, among others. These names illustrate the fondness of coiners of slang for rhyme and alliteration.

Slang includes many figures of speech beside euphemism. The most common is metaphor. It is often possible to notice a semantic parallel between a slang word and a quite different standard English word. The original meaning of the verb *to insult* was 'to jump on' and slang uses *jump on* in the same metaphorical sense. *To catch on* in the sense 'to understand' is now rather old-fashioned slang, but it is the same metaphor as that found in the equally old-fashioned standard English *apprehend*. Standard English *supercilious* is derived from the Latin *supercilium* (eyebrow), and we can see in the word the same association of ideas that underlies the use of the word *highbrow*. When we say that someone is *recalcitrant*, we are using the same metaphor that the speaker of slang would use if he said that he was *a kicker*.

In the creation of slang words two opposing tendencies can be seen at work. There is, first of all, a love of conciseness. Long words are shortened: *business* becomes *biz*; *lunatic* becomes *loony*; *influenza* becomes *flu*. Some of these curtailments have been accepted as standard English and have virtually replaced the longer words from which they are derived: *cabriolet* has been replaced by *cab* and *omnibus* by *bus*. But side by side with this trend towards conciseness there is a love of exuberance, which creates words like *bobby-dazzler*. Both tendencies may affect the same word. *O.K.* owes much of its popularity to its brevity, and lovers of brevity reduce it further to a single syllable *oke*. Beyond this it cannot go, but lovers of slang don't like things to stay as they are, and so elaboration sets to work and *oke* becomes *okey-doke*. *Pepper* is shortened to *pep* and given the new sense 'vigour, energy'. The shortened form is used in *pep-talk*, a speech intended to keep up morale or to stimulate to action. *Popular* is shortened to *pop* and this serves as the first element of a compound in *pop-singer*.

Blend-words, of the kind that Lewis Carroll called portmanteau words, are not uncommon in slang. Lewis Carroll's poem *Jabberwocky* has given us *chortle*, and Sir Alan Herbert's Topsy has contributed *equibiguous* from *equivocal* and *ambiguous*. *Mummersetshire* is a happy term for the hybrid stage form of speech used in dialect plays by authors who are not themselves dialect speakers. The suffix -*er* is often used in the formation of slang words. The term *has-been* to describe a man who is past his best, on occasion calls for something stronger, and the call is answered by *never-waser*. In northern towns, before the days of alarm-clocks, a well-known benefactor was the man who went round the town in the early morning wakening those who had to go to work early. He was known as a *knocker-upper*, with a double suffix.

Two world wars have done much to increase the use of slang. They have done this partly by changing our attitude towards slang and partly by the introduction of new words to describe war-time conditions. Slang was much used by members of the armed forces and they spread many slang words among civilians. Slang flourishes on informality, and in time of war informal occasions are numerous. No rigid division between formal and informal occasions is possible, and we now hear slang from time to time from the most formal persons, though when a man of formal habits uses slang it is sometimes possible to detect the quotations marks in his voice. Slang words to become popular during the First World War include *Blighty* (England), *brass hat* (high-ranking officer), *cushy* (comfortable) and *windy* (afraid). The *wangler* of the First World War became the *spiv* of the Second, and both of them sometimes achieved their ends by *fiddling*. From the Second World War we have *blitz* (air-raid), with its more or less facetious derivatives *blitzlet* (minor raid), *day-blitz* (raid during the daytime) and *off-blitz* (night when no raid took place). *Quisling* (traitor) may perhaps be regarded as standard English, but the same cannot be said for such derivatives as *de-quizzle* (to put a car out of action so that no Quisling could use it).

The task of distinguishing between slang and dialect becomes difficult when groups of people develop their own slang. Every occupation tends to develop a special vocabulary, some of which consists of technical terms that may be used in textbooks or on formal occasions while other words are clearly slang. Repairers of radio sets often refer to a valve as a *bottle*, and hence *bottle-changer* becomes a natural term for an unskilled man who can change a valve but is incapable of anything more difficult. It is not uncommon for a man employed by a firm to undertake extra work on his own account. Extra jobs of this kind are known as *foreigners*. The freedom with which slang is used in any occupation depends on the extent to which those who follow it behave as a group. Farmers are individualists and so use little slang, but actors use a good deal. Some theatrical slang has passed into everyday English and its theatrical origin is forgotten. *Claptrap* is simply a trap to catch applause. It is today used of public speakers more often than of actors, but it derives its meaning from the theatrical custom of clapping the hands to express approval. *Blue gags* are salacious jokes, so called, no doubt, because they are liable to be removed by the censor's blue pencil. Actors have to face long periods of unemployment, for which different euphemisms are used on the two sides of the Atlantic: an American actor is *at liberty* while a British actor is *resting*. Feeble jests are described as *corny*, and an inferior actor is called a *ham*. Granville[1] says that barnstorming actors used ham fat as a make-up base or remover, *barnstormer* is itself a piece of theatrical slang, going back to the days when there was less competition from cinema and television than there is today. Touring companies rented barns in which they gave performances where restraint was not regarded as a virtue. A theatre or a cinema which charges low prices is liable to be known as a *flea-pit*. When a play is not going very well a lavish distribution of complimentary tickets may disguise the fact; such a distribution is described as *papering the house*. It is unnecessary if the actors are popular; such actors are sometimes said to be *box-office*. The best of plays need financial backing, often provided by men outside the theatrical profession. They are gratefully known as *angels* and they are sometimes said to *angel the show*. The same readiness to use one part of speech for another is seen in the expression *to ad-lib* to describe the improvisation that becomes necessary when an actor misses his entrance cue. To under-stress a cue-line has the effect of spoiling a fellow-actor's next line, which loses much of its point if the cue is not heard by the audience. This practice is known as *biting cues*. A number of more or less derisive nouns are coined by the addition of *-y* or *-ie* to a common word: a *biggy* is a star actor; a *weepy* is a sentimental play, sometimes known as a *tear-jerker*; a *baddy* is a villain and a

[1] *A Dictionary of Theatrical Terms*, p. 95.

goody is a hero. Some theatrical slang shows cynicism, as when a play or a part is described as *actor-proof* or *audience-proof*, so good that no actor or audience can wreck it. There are phrases that are much used. The meaning of *I had 'em in the aisles* is clear: the audience laughed so much that they fell out of their seats. Less obvious but very well known is *The ghost walks on Friday*, meaning that Friday is pay-day. The origin is said to have been Hamlet's reference to his father's ghost: 'Perchance 'twill walk again.' An actor playing the ghost shouted back from the wings: 'I'll be damned if he will unless our salaries are paid.' Other jokes or pleasantries are preserved in phrases. *A thinking part* is a walk-on part; the actor has nothing to say but it is presumed that he thinks a lot. Another is *whisky-stall* to describe a stall at the end of a row from which the bar is easily accessible. In the theatre *to dry* means 'to forget one's lines' and *to strike* means 'to take down scenery'. Sometimes the understanding of a phrase demands a knowledge of the theatrical conventions of a particular period. For example, the phrase *broker's men* is used to describe the two comedians whose act is one of the conventions of the British pantomime. A comedian may depend a good deal on the co-operation of another actor who is willing to be a target for his gags. Such an actor is known as a *feed* or a *stooge*. The latter word has come to be used of anyone who performs a subordinate role. American English *double-talk* is theatrical slang for meaningless talk that appears to make sense. It is also used of people who insincerely say one thing while meaning another.

It is natural that many of the slang words current today have to do with drug addiction. Since it is illegal to sell or possess certain drugs, those who traffic in them have good reason to develop their own secret language, and the people who take drugs are often those who would in any case make free use of slang. We thus have *grass* for hashish, and *mainline* (to take narcotics intravenously), *to push* (to peddle drugs) and *trip* to describe the state of hallucination induced by a drug. A man under the influence of a drug is *high* or *turned on* or *stoned*. If he becomes dependent on drugs he is said to be *hooked*. A drug that is not habit-forming is said to be *soft*, while the drug known as *LSD* is, among others, described as *acid*.

6

Usage

MANY people act on the assumption that there are only two varieties of English: good and bad. It is the purpose of this book to suggest that this view is mistaken, but any account of the varieties of English would be incomplete if it failed to consider how far 'correct English' can be accepted as one of the many varieties that exist.

The whole idea of correctness in linguistic matters is under fire. For years schoolboys and adults without much schooling have been using expressions like 'these sort of people' or 'a gastric stomach', and have looked suitably abashed when their attention has been called to the lack of concord or when they have been asked what other sort of stomach is possible. The change that has come about is that they no longer look abashed. They can count on allies in high places who will assure them that usage is the only test of correctness and that if a mistake is made often enough it ceases to be a mistake at all. The very natural satisfaction which linguistic innovators feel on receiving such support may turn out to be short-lived. Like so many things, it is largely a matter of terminology. The schoolboy, relieved from the burden of deciding what is correct, may feel that he is little better off when he is told that certain phrases are 'not socially acceptable', and there are resemblances in meaning between the old-fashioned adjective 'illiterate' and the term 'substandard' which even up-to-date linguists allow themselves to use, though they sometimes wince when doing so.

One thing that makes the use of the English language difficult is that people are continually inventing new sins. The inventors are often men of high prestige, and when they call attention to breaches of the laws that they have themselves created, the tendency in the past has been to accept their castigation and to try to reform. In recent years a reaction has set in, and there are many writers, including some whose opinions demand respect, who say that questions of right and wrong have no place in linguistic matters and that it is merely a question of usage. They wish us to follow the advice of Mr Pickwick and, when we find two crowds shouting contradictory opinions, they say that we should shout with the larger.

It is salutary to ask whether the linguistic sins of which people complain are in fact sins at all, and conversely, when one particular variety of English is praised it is well to ask not only whether it possesses the qualities that are claimed for it, but also whether those qualities are in fact virtues. R. W. Chapman wrote an S.P.E. Tract on ' *Oxford' English*, in the course of which he said :

> Even our grammar is threatened. The traditional use of *shall* and *will* is not much understood or practised outside the limits of standard English, and is certainly in danger: not only in danger of being swamped but in danger of direct assault.[1]

The traditional use of *shall* and *will* may be in danger, but the important question is whether it is worth preserving.

Among the imaginary sins which have been the subject of reproof in the past we may include the use of loan-words instead of words of native origin, the use of hybrids where different parts of the same word are borrowed from different languages, and the failure to pronounce loan-words as they were pronounced in the language from which they are borrowed. The last reproach is often based on half-knowledge. The word *cinema* is derived ultimately from a Greek word beginning with *k-*, but that is not sufficient reason for pronouncing it with [k]. We have to ask also whether it was borrowed directly from Greek or through French, where the *c* was pronounced [s]. Another relevant question is: does the pronunciation with [k] harmonise with the usual English pronunciation of *c* before front vowels? If it does not, by using [k] we are preserving an inconsistency which adds to the already considerable difficulty of English spelling. The usual English practice is to anglicise the pronunciation of loan-words which have been in the language long enough to become familiar.

[1] S.P.E. Tract No. 37 (1932).

Another subject of reproach among those who complain that the English language is going to the dogs is that a particular usage is of American origin. But if a word or a syntactic construction is generally understood, it is the height of folly to single out a particular part of the English-speaking community and to say that usages that had their origin there must not be allowed to spread. To the student of the history of the English language it is a matter of interest to know which linguistic usages had their origin in the United States, but to the man who wants to use the language American origin is unimportant.

We have gone too far in our fear of being prescriptive. Usage is only one of the things that we should keep in mind when deciding whether to use one word or another. Usage is important, but an important aspect of the question is 'Whose usage?' The usage that matters most is that of the individual or the group that we are talking to. It is desirable that we should use the variety of English with which they are most familiar without diverging too much from that which they expect us to use, if there is any difference between the two varieties. The reason for such conformity is obvious: it avoids distracting the attention of our hearers from what we are saying to our way of saying it. But there are other requirements that may conflict with usage. One is that useful distinctions of meaning should be preserved. Another objective worth aiming at is simplicity. It is desirable that ideas should, if necessary, be complicated but the expression of those ideas should be simple, whereas too often the converse is true.

In linguistic matters it is entirely healthy that philologists should insist that their business is to record and explain what happens rather than to prescribe what should happen, but it is well to remember that the philologist is not the only person who is concerned with language. Language is an aspect of human behaviour, and all human beings and all those who teach them are entitled to demand that their views should be taken into account. There are clear advantages in uniformity of spelling, and a speaker who, like Humpty Dumpty, gives words meanings of his own choice or who fails to speak clearly is going to be a nuisance to his hearers, no matter what parallels a philologist may be able to quote for his linguistic eccentricities. There is a parallel between a philologist's attitude towards language and that of a botanist towards flowers: both philologist and botanist are likely to be more interested in the wild than in the cultivated varieties. There are others, however, whose attitude is different. The gardener imposes a pattern on his flowers and the schoolmaster imposes a pattern on the speech of his pupils. Those who are neither philologists nor schoolmasters find the speech of others a useful guide to their personality. Does this stranger use the same sort of clichés as we use ourselves? Is he well disposed towards us? Is he going to bore us by talking too much or talking too little? There are many words and phrases which are not in themselves either right or wrong but which are valuable chiefly as symptoms. Those who are interested in the social graces will notice whether a stranger says 'Pleased to meet you' on being introduced or 'Cheers' when drinking. Those who are more interested in the question 'Can he be a sensible man?' have a more difficult question to answer. It is a part of the sadness of human life that many of the linguistic indicators that most often cause this question to be answered in the negative are the result of an attempt to make a good impression. Fowler's comment on *galore* could apply to a good many words; he says that the word is 'chiefly resorted to by those who are reduced to relieving dullness of matter by oddity of expression.'[1]

The term 'correct' is not a good one to use in describing language. It is very rarely true to say that one word is right and that all others are worng. This does not mean that it does not matter how we speak or how we behave. One word may be demonstrably better than another even though it cannot be claimed that it is absolutely right. Moreover speech, like other kinds of conduct, is revealing. By his choice of words a man shows himself to be either fastidious or careless.

The permissiveness which is fashionable in linguistic matters today is to be welcomed in that it is a move away from the state of things where everything that is not forbidden is compulsory, and it may make life easier for the man whose only object is to have an easy life, but it makes life more rather than less difficult for the man who wishes to write and speak well. So long as the effective use of language is a matter of memoris-

[1] H. W. Fowler, *A Dictionary of Modern English Usage.* (O.U.P., 1926) p. 210.

ing and applying rules, there is no scope for the outstanding achievement that demands outstanding effort. We do not congratulate a man on the excellence of his spelling, however superb it may be. But though permissiveness makes good speaking and writing more difficult, it also makes it more enjoyable. The difficulty is a challenge.

A good approach to the problem of usage is to apply the test of appropriateness: good English is English that is appropriate to its purpose in a particular situation. It has been objected that this approach to language leads to the decline of a general and reputable usage and adds greatly to the difficulty of using a language, since a speaker does not often know the linguistic habits of his hearers well enough to adapt his speech to them. Another objection is that a speaker, and even more a writer, may be addressing a large audience of very different speech-habits. Only when speaking to an individual whom one knows well can one hope to speak in a way that will seem completely appropriate and, far from being grateful, the hearer is liable to feel that he is being talked down to. Mr Knightley, in Jane Austen's *Emma*, was very resentful at the idea of Frank Churchill adapting himself to his hearers in this way (chap. 18). On the other hand, a completely consistent adherence to the idea of general usage, rejecting attempts at appropriateness, would have the effect of producing a fixed language inadmissive of improvement. The history of languages shows that change is inevitable, and changes that eventually become generally accepted begin as the eccentricities of individuals.

Compromise is clearly called for. It is well to accept that complete appropriateness of language is unattainable, but that is no reason why we should give up the attempt completely. It is reasonable that we should try to avoid jarring on the linguistic susceptibilities of our hearers either by 'talking lah-di-dah' or by using words that they do not understand or that they regard as vulgarisms. On the other hand, a speaker need not feel bound to use a turn of phrase that he himself dislikes just because he knows that his hearers are unlikely to share his views. And harmony with the linguistic habits of one's hearers is only one kind of appropriateness. A speaker or a writer should also try to use language appropriate to his subject matter.

Standard English is sometimes defined as the speech which is least likely to attract attention to itself as being peculiar to any class or locality. The objection to this definition is that the likelihood of attracting attention to itself depends on environment. In a Yorkshire mining village standard English would be more likely to attract attention as being peculiar than would the dialect of the village.

The appeal to usage is most often made in support of greater permissiveness, but it can work both ways. It would be perfectly easy to justify *mouses* as a plural of *mouse* by invoking analogy and quoting parallels such as *cows*, which has replaced the historically correct plural *kye* (O.E. *cū*, sg.; *cȳ*, pl.), but as a matter of usage we know that in the particular word *mouse* the historically defensible analogy has not taken place. The objection to clumsy expression is that it wastes the time of the listener or reader. The reader can usually puzzle out the author's meaning by pausing or re-reading. The listener has not these advantages and he therefore fails to grasp the author's exact meaning.

There are widespread misconceptions about the part which dictionaries should play in matters of usage. There are several books dealing with English usage which not only describe what is the usual practice but also recommend which usage is to be preferred. Books of this kind are often arranged alphabetically for ease of reference and they may be called dictionaries. The best-known book of this kind is Fowler's *Dictionary of Modern English Usage* (O.U.P., 1926), of which a revised edition has been published, edited by Sir Ernest Gowers (1965). Such books, however, are not typical dictionaries. The primary function of a dictionary is to record what a substantial number of speakers and writers do, not what the editor of the dictionary thinks that they ought to do. This conception of the function of a dictionary was not accepted by a Manchester merchant, who approached the publishers or editors of nineteen dictionaries to protest against the inclusion of such definitions of *Jew* as 'usurer', 'miser' and 'extortionate tradesman'. The publishers of some of the dictionaries promised to re-word their definition in future editions, but the publishers of one resisted:

We must stand firm as the function of a dictionary is purely to record how words are actually used.

The fact remains that Gentiles of a certain background and degree of insensitivity do use the word casually to mean a miser, without thought for the etymology of the word.

While this practice persists, we shall continue to retain the entry.

The objector was not satisfied with this reply (*Daily Telegraph*, 4 April 1970), but it would find many supporters. A compromise is possible. Dictionaries not only may but should record widely current meanings of words even if the editor thinks them offensive, but it is possible for the editor of a dictionary to add comments like 'Not now in polite use', and foreigners using English dictionaries have expressed the wish that their compilers would include such comments more freely.

One comment that is often used in dictionaries is 'colloquial', but this label is sometimes omitted on the grounds that its use may make some people think that the expression so described is to be avoided altogether. Such an assumption is unjustified. A colloquialism is not a second-best word or phrase to be used only if the speaker cannot think of a more formal way of expressing his ideas; on many occasions it is to be preferred to a more formal expression. As the etymology of the word implies, a colloquialism is appropriate to conversation, but even in the written language colloquialisms can be very effective if they are used with tact. One reason why the articles written by American academics are often so readable is that their authors will sometimes relieve the formal style of an academic essay by colloquialisms. More serious objection could be taken to descriptions like 'incorrect' or 'erroneous'. One might perhaps use the word 'erroneous' to describe a misquotation, as in the telescoped phrase 'to gild the lily,'[1] but even here those guilty of a misquotation have been known to plead usage as though it were a complete justification. As a rule, however, the distinction is not between right and wrong, but in degrees of appropriateness, and it is here that we should be prepared to fight a rearguard action against those who believe that usage should be the only criterion.

There is a popular party game which requires the contestants

---

[1] 'To gild refined gold, to paint the lily . . . Is wasteful and ridiculous excess' (*King John*, IV ii *II*).

to make an impromptu speech lasting a minute without hesitation, repetition or deviation from the subject. When the game is played as a radio panel game the contestants are usually actors, and it is interesting to see how rarely even trained performers manage to talk for a minute without being successfully challenged. The discipline of the rules of this game could very profitably be extended to public speakers, but it would be a disaster if it were extended to conversation. The charm of conversation lies in the readiness to pass quickly from one subject to another, and though a speech lasting for a minute might be tolerated as a rare exception, any conversationalist who made a habit of speaking for a minute at a time would be regarded as a bore. In conversation, hesitation is welcomed because it gives an unwilling listener a chance to interrupt.

Lightness of touch is a quality that comes naturally to some speakers and writers but, if it does not, it is not easy to acquire. It is lost by a speaker who thinks that the points that he makes are so important that he must not take the risk that any of them will be missed. A writer is in greater danger than a speaker of labouring his points, because he cannot tell by the facial expression of his readers whether they have understood him. A teacher gets into the way of noticing those of his students who have mobile faces and whose capacity he knows. If they all show signs of understanding all that he says, he can be sure that some of his hearers will be bored by his slowness.

There is a tendency sometimes to disparage the art of writing as something 'merely verbal', a technique that has its uses but not a matter of first importance. Reports have to be written, but the art of writing them is assumed to be a minor accomplishment that can be undertaken by an underling who is given the task of 'putting that into good English'. In fact, good expression grows naturally out of the subject-matter; it is not something to be sprinkled on afterwards. Unless a writer can express his ideas clearly, one is entitled to doubt whether he himself has thought them out fully.

One of the problems of communication arises from the fact that many people do not listen very closely to what other people have to say. If charged with this breach of good manners, they might reply that most of what is said in casual conversation does not deserve very close attention and that it is a waste of time to puzzle out the exact meaning of words which a speaker has not chosen with any great care. When we are talking to people whom we know well, we almost unconsciously get into the habit of learning which of our acquaintances choose their words carefully and therefore deserve close attention. Perhaps one of the most common remarks in the recriminatory quarrels in which some people delight is 'That is what you implied'. Implication is a perfectly valid means of communication. For example, if a government department issues a warning that interest will be charged on overdue tax of more than £1,000, there is a clear implication that it will not be charged on amounts of less than £1,000. But a charge of implication usually means that the words implied are what the hearer expected and what he chooses to assume was the intended meaning.

Advice on choice of words is often given to those who wish to write. They are advised, for example, to prefer the concrete to the abstract, the short word to the long, and the Saxon word to one of Romance origin. Such advice may do more harm than good because it is liable to be taken too seriously. Any such advice should include the important proviso that the two words in question must express the writer's meaning equally well. It would be absurd to sacrifice some of the richness of the English vocabulary by rejecting a generally understood Romance word on the grounds that there is a native near-synonym. What the author has to decide is which word has for him the right associations to express his meaning as exactly as possible. That choice is in itself so difficult that there is no point in making the task harder by applying a set of rules. There is, however, one rule that every writer should remember: to choose words that his reader is likely to be able to understand. This advice is not easy to follow, because the writer of a book or an article is writing for a group that is not homogeneous, but it is bad manners for an author to parade his own learning at the expense of his readers.

Vague words like *situation, position, state of affairs* are often used from laziness. A little thought would enable the speaker to say what is the special aspect of the situation to which he wishes to call attention, but he prefers to leave the listener to do his work for him. Cowardice is another motive for vagueness:

if a speaker described the situation more precisely, it might be that someone would disagree with him. If he is vague, there is nothing with which anyone can either agree or disagree. In much the same way an author may write 'It is significant that . . .', hoping that the reader will have ideas about the significance of the remark that he will charitably attribute to the writer. It is the writer's business to say what is the significance of the fact to which he calls attention. On the other hand, the authors of books on the writing of English are liable to suffer from attacks of pedantry which make them try to attach precise meanings to words and phrases which enjoy wide currency simply because they are vague. Thus, Graves and Hodge[1] have a table of nineteen different percentages ranging from 0 per cent to 100 per cent, which they take to be the meanings of such phrases as 'a small part' (15 per cent), 'part' (25 per cent), 'a considerable part' (30 per cent) and 'quite a large part' (35 per cent). If anyone attaches to any of these phrases a different percentage they assume that he has made a mistake which needs correction. Such precision is both unattainable and unnecessary.

It would be going too far to say that we should never use clichés. For one thing it is not always easy to say at what point an idiom becomes a cliché. There is a sense in which every word in the language is a quotation, and a quotation excessively used becomes a cliché. We are content to use the vocabulary that has been invented and handed down by others and there is no reason why we should reject phrases that are generally understood and that express our meaning precisely, even if their usefulness has led to their use many thousands of times previously. The danger is that the excessive use of clichés can become a substitute for thought. Sir Ernest Gowers says of what he calls 'pudder':

> Instead of being simple, terse and direct, it is stilted, long-winded, and circumlocutory; instead of the plain phrase the cliché. . . . It is as though the builder of a house did not take the trouble to select with care the materials that he

[1] Robert Graves and Alan Hodge, *The Reader over Your Shoulder* (Cape, 1943) p. 140.

thought most suitable for his purpose, but collected chunks of masonry from ruined houses built by others, and stuck them together anyhow. That is not a promising way to produce anything significant in meaning, attractive in form, or of any practical use.

The Complete Plain Words, chap. 5

One objection to 'gobbledygook' (as it is called in America) is that to the untrained ear (including that of the user) it is liable to seem more impressive than simple language.

Clichés are used frequently because they describe situations that recur frequently; they become objectionable when they become a substitute for thought. It is very easy to feel that we have solved a problem when we have merely described it in a familiar phrase. The legitimate use of a cliché is similar to that of an end-game in chess. When a familiar situation recurs it is not necessary to play the game out every time. Everyone concerned knows what the result would be.

Clichés sometimes lead to the use of needlessly strong language. The expression *a diabolical liberty* is often used in contexts where such strong language is not really justified. It was used, for example, by different speakers to describe an increase of twopence in the price of beer and an unwelcome change in a radio programme.

Some words express praise or blame according to varying estimates of the qualities they describe. It is not uncommon in the senior common rooms of universities to hear a subject dismissed as 'of merely academic importance'. The speakers are unconsciously accepting the low opinion of academic activity that is held by many non-academics. The names of religious sects or political parties have often been accepted with pride by those to whom they have been applied in scorn. Thus we have Lollards and Quakers, Whigs and Tories. Some words are unexpectedly pejorative. To do good, to take an interest in culture, to be interested in things of the mind and to have a strong moral sense are not in themselves reprehensible, yet the terms *do-gooder*, *culture vulture*, *highbrow* and *prig* are terms of abuse. They may have acquired the status because admirable qualities are liable to be disparaged by those who do not possess them, but words of this kind often imply the possession of some less admirable quality. A do-gooder is thought of as ineffective and a culture vulture as one who is anxious to make a good impression; a highbrow has been defined as a man educated beyond his intelligence and a prig applies his moral standards unreasonably.

It is a very good habit to get into the way of defining the terms that we use, even if we only do it to ourselves, and it is often surprisingly difficult. It need cause us no surprise if the definition of quite a simple word turns out to be complicated. A common piece of schoolboy whimsy is to ask someone to define a spiral staircase, in order to find out how many people have to resort to gesture language accompanied by some vague phrase like 'A thing that goes round and round'. One exception to this common type of reply was provided by a man who replied with quiet confidence: 'A circle with an upward tendency.'

The rest of this chapter is devoted to a discussion of some specific points of usage by way of illustration of the problems that a speaker or writer must face. The examples are taken from the three fields of vocabulary, word-formation and syntax.

When we are trying to decide whether to make a distinction between two words of similar meaning, two questions have to be asked. The first is: is the distinction worth making? The second is: once the distinction is made, can our hearers be expected to understand and remember it? The distinction between *disinterested* (free from bias) and *uninterested* (not interested) is an important one, which is worth preserving. On the other hand, when several speakers were asked to say whether they used the spelling *grey* or *gray*, some of them replied that the two spellings indicated to them two different shades of the colour. Here we have to ask whether all of those who make a distinction make the same distinction and whether it is worth while trying to remember what differences particular speakers see in the two spellings, which for most people do not represent different shades.

Writers have to beware of using idioms that are capable of a double meaning. Anyone who is accustomed to using statistics knows the necessity of breaking down large groups into more homogeneous subdivisions. At the same time one is conscious of something that could have been better expressed in a table of statistics which has the heading: 'Adult Population of Great Britain Broken Down by Age and Sex'. Again, one cannot be entirely satisfied with the wording of an advertisement which states that a boarding-school has a 'strong language side'. Which of the two nouns does the adjective qualify?

Familiar words may have associations for particular groups of hearers that are quite unsuspected by those who use them. An Englishman travelling in the United States made a speech to express his appreciation of the hospitality that he had received. He said 'In my own country I should have said you have given me a royal welcome, though in this country I suppose I should say that you have given me a republican welcome.' The deathly silence with which this quip was received clearly had some deeper cause than boredom. Fortunately the speaker recollected that he was in a Southern state and he therefore went on: 'or rather, I should say, a democratic welcome'. Loud applause.

The desire to achieve emphasis leads to the use of *literally* in the sense 'metaphorically', a usage which causes great joy to many connoisseurs, who can be found storing up examples to exchange with other collectors. Most metaphors are faded with excessive use, and a speaker in search of emphasis will sometimes claim quite legitimately that what he is saying is no mere metaphor: it is the literal truth. But the legitimate uses of the word are heavily outnumbered by the illegitimate, where the speaker has lost all thought of the meaning of the word and uses it in an attempt to be impressive, just as some writers use exclamation marks. A motorist, delayed by rush-hour traffic, will claim that he literally crawled home, and the winner of a tennis match has been described as having literally wiped the floor with his opponent.

Some writers have the habit of introducing each new idea by some phrase like *It is important to note that*. Such phrases are better omitted, although they sometimes have a legitimate use. For example, *For your information* can properly be used to distinguish a letter that calls for action from one that does not. It is often used without this distinction, and it is sometimes used to introduce an offensive remark.

Of course is used to placate a reader who may complain that the writer is saying something obvious, but if a remark is so obvious as to justify the use of *of course*, it is quite likely that it could with advantage be omitted altogether. The same is true of *obviously*, while *fairly obviously* is patronising.

It has been said that the adjective is the enemy of the noun. If we get into the habit of using adjectives to express ideas that are already implicit in the nouns they qualify, the meaning of the noun is weakened. The danger is not so much with adjectives that are obviously tautological; only an unskilful writer refers to a *new innovation* or *green verdure*. It is rather with adjectives that are used merely for emphasis: *a real danger*, *a terrible catastrophe*. The proper function of adjectives is to make the meaning of nouns more precise, not to emphasise them. If adjectives are habitually used to emphasise nouns, we have the usual result of over-emphasis: the meaning of the noun is weakened and we are left with no good way of indicating emphasis on the few occasions when it is really necessary. Certain nouns tend to be used with particular adjectives. *Consideration* is usually *active*. The reason for the linking of the two words is that *under consideration* has been used so often to indicate indefinite delay that *active* is inserted as a reassurance: we really are thinking about the matter. There is a similar tendency to use adverbs needlessly. It is not necessary to say that a thing is *relatively large*, since the adverb *relatively* is implicit in the meaning of adjectives like *large* and *small*.

Technical terms are often misused. *By and large* is often used in the sense 'broadly speaking', but it is a precise steering order to a helmsman, given according to the direction of wind relative to the desired course. *He disappeared at a speed of knots per hour* is doubly wrong: *knots* indicate speed without the addition *per hour* and, unless the number of knots is indicated, the sentence tells us nothing about the speed.

Meanings that are frowned on include *mutual* in the sense of 'common'. Reluctance to say *common* may be due to the ambiguity of the word, which is often used pejoratively. Dickens's use of *mutual* in the title *Our Mutual Friend* has done much to encourage the use of the word in the sense 'common'. There has been a constant search for words to indicate a human being of either sex. *Wight* is archaic; *person* is sometimes used pejoratively, *individual* was much used in Victorian times, but it is open to the objection that it sometimes serves a useful purpose to distinguish a person from a corporate body. *Aggravating* for *annoying* is an example of specialisation to which many parallels could be cited, but by an accident of usage it has come to be regarded by many people as a vulgarism. *Anticipate* is often used with the sense 'expect'. Here too, the earlier use of *anticipate* tends to be lost in consequence. What is the meaning of the sentence: 'John and Mary anticipated their marriage with great pleasure?' The distinction between *infer* and *imply* is becoming blurred but it is worth preserving: a speaker implies what his hearer infers.

One distinction that is made by purists but not by the man in the street is that between *less* and *fewer*. The purist will use *fewer* of numbers but *less* of size; the ordinary man will get along without using the word *fewer* at all, but will say 'There are less people here than there were last week'. The use of *fewer* is generally regarded as a sign of the academic, as in the remark attributed to a professor watching a game of rugby football: 'And I am told that many of the players have fewer than a thousand volumes.'

The use of different suffixes may introduce variations of meaning that are worth preserving. *Historical* means 'connected with history'; *historic* means 'noted in history'. *Economic* means 'connected with economics'; *economical* means 'frugal'. Some suffixes are thought to be pejorative; for this reason, since the Second World War *Asiatic* has tended to be replaced by *Asian*. A form with a suffix is often more pejorative than the simple word; examples are *visit(ation)*, *sentiment(ality)*, *Methodist(ical)*.

Some speakers are fond of the figure of speech known as litotes, which expresses an idea as the negative of its contrary. As a mannerism this can become tiresome, and George Orwell poured scorn on it by suggesting that those who suffer from the disease should memorise the sentence 'A not unblack dog was chasing a not unsmall rabbit across a not ungreen field'.[1] This is not quite fair. The use of *not un-* is especially popular with adjectives like *interesting* and *welcome*, which do not admit of precise measurement. *Not uninteresting* does not mean the same as *interesting*. There is a large intermediate category of

[1] Gowers, *The Complete Plain Words*, p. 76.

things that are not clearly either uninteresting or interesting. *Interesting* excludes this intermediate group; *not uninteresting* includes it.

The decay of English inflections has been carried so far that the few that remain have their backs to the wall. The inflected form *whom* is on the way out, and anyone who says *who* when *whom* is grammatically correct can count on the silent approval of most of the small number of his hearers who will notice the substitution. What has to be avoided is the converse use of *whom* for *who*. By using *whom* at all a speaker puts himself among those who are particular about details of usage and, if he uses it incorrectly, he will have to face not only the disapproval of the purists but the derision of the much larger number of people who care nothing for linguistic minutiae but who do dislike anyone who tries to be clever, especially if he shows himself to be ignorant of the rules which he is trying to foist on his fellow-men. *Whom* is used so rarely that one is unable to rely on the usual test 'Does it sound right?' but a useful test is to substitute for *who(m)* the subjective and objective cases of the personal pronoun, which are so common that most people can quickly decide which is preferable. The use of *whom* for *who* is most liable to take place in fairly long sentences, when *who* is preceded by a preposition or a transitive verb as in *She had not the vaguest idea of whom he might be*. Another cause of the mistaken use of *whom* for *who* is that the offender may in his youth have devoted more time to the study of Latin than of English grammar and may be influenced by the Latin accusative and infinitive construction. In the sentence *This is the man whom they thought to be drowned*, *whom* is justifiable, and it is an easy matter to introduce it into the sentence *This is the man who they thought was drowned*.

A participle or participial phrase normally refers to the subject of the sentence in which it occurs. An unattached participle is one that can find no word in the sentence with which it can agree, while satisfying the demands of grammar and expressing the author's meaning. An example is: *Having decided to leave the party early, the problem was how to get away*. Before condemning an unattached participle one has to remember two possibilities. The first is that in course of time certain participles and adjectives have come to be used as prepositions. In a phrase like *considering the circumstances*, it is reasonable to regard *considering* as a preposition meaning 'in view of'. Reasonable but not universal. Many people deplore the growing tendency to use *following* as a preposition meaning 'after', and there is even stronger opposition to the use of *due to* and *owing to* as prepositional phrases meaning 'on account of' or 'because of' in sentences like *Due to a bad cold, he couldn't come*. The second point about the use of participles is that it is quite permissible to use a participle in an absolute construction, which stands outside the normal syntactic construction of a sentence. One could say, for example, *The party being over, he went home*.

One special use of participles is that known as the 'fused participle'. This construction results from the use of the suffix *-ing* to represent both a present participle and a verbal noun. *There can be no objection to your coming* illustrates the use of *coming* as a verbal noun, which normally requires the possessive adjective *your*. There is, however, a growing tendency in colloquial speech to replace *your* by *you*, and *coming* is then described as a fused participle. H. W. Fowler's objection that this construction 'defies grammatical analysis' is hardly final; it is the business of grammatical analysis to record the facts of language, not to mould them to its will, and the fused participle has become one of the facts of the English language. The case against it was put by H. W. Fowler in S.P.E. Tract No. 22 (1925) and the case for it was presented at some length by Otto Jespersen in S.P.E. Tract No. 25 (1926).

Some people object to the use of *very* with a past participle, as in phrases like *very tired* or *very pleased*, but if a word, originally a participle, has become an adjective and is used without any thought of the verb from which it is derived, it is pedantic to object to the use of *very*.

English prepositions have a wide range of meanings, and one sometimes has the choice of several different prepositions to express a single idea. The writer of the following sentence would have done better to use *about* instead of *of* in order to make it clear that the wild-eyed eight-year-olds were not the audience but the subject of complaint:

He had told the meeting of wild-eyed eight-year-olds biting their teachers, of nine-year-olds spitting and using obscene

language, and of class teachers having to join forces to
separate screaming girls.

Daily Telegraph, 16 February 1968

A desire to avoid giving offence by overlooking anybody
sometimes leads to a needlessly clumsy sentence. One parson
is said to have modified a well-known Biblical text to read

> Greater love has no man (or woman) than this, that a man
> (or woman) lay down his (or her) life for his (or her) friends.

The simplest solution of the problem is to assume that the
masculine pronoun can be used to refer to both men and
women. Ambiguity sometimes arises from the use of nouns like
'cousin', 'student' or 'advertiser' that can refer to either men
or women. No doubt such a use of the noun 'collector' explains the apparently invidious practice of auctioneers who will
describe one lot as 'the property of a gentleman' and another
as 'the property of a collector'. The second lot may be offered
for sale by a woman who thinks that her sex is no business of the
auctioneer or the bidders.

When usage conflicts with what has hitherto been regarded
as a grammatical rule, it is reasonable to examine the context
of the apparent breach of rule to see whether the breach is due
to some conflicting principle which may justify us in saying that
it should be not only tolerated but preferred. In general it is
sound advice to put adverbs like *only* as near as possible to the
words they modify, yet to follow this advice often conflicts
with what seems to most of us the natural way of speaking.
To say *I want only three* demands conscious effort; left to ourselves, most of us would say *I only want three*. The latter construction has been defended:

> The intention of the speaker may be to emphasize the
> reasonableness of his request, not the request itself or the
> exact amount being requested. If such is his intention, the
> sooner he introduces the idea of reasonableness into his
> expression the truer he is to his actual meaning and the more
> likely he is to get a favorable response.[1]

[1] Charles V. Hartung, 'Doctrines of English Usage', *English Journal*, XLV
(1956). Quoted from *Essays on Language and Usage*, ed. Leonard F. Dean and
Kenneth G. Wilson, 2nd ed. (New York: O.U.P., 1963) p. 266.

Certain departures from normal English syntax do not come naturally but result from attempts to avoid what seem to the speakers to be mistakes. The consciousness that grammarians prescribe *whom* in sentences where most people say *who* leads many uneasy users of English to say or write *whom* without grammatical justification. Similarly, fear of saying *It's me* leads many people to feel that the subjective case of pronouns is in some way more respectable than the objective, with the result that we get *between you and I*.

Some departures from the linguistic norm show that the speaker has a little learning but not enough. Nouns of the Latin second declension, having -*i* in the nominative plural, are sometimes imported into English and keep their Latin plural forms as in *radii*; the writer who uses plurals like *ignorami* and *octopi* has failed to recognise that *ignoramus* is a verb and that the *us* of *octopus* is not an inflexional ending. Those who know the length of vowels in Latin or Greek loan-words into English sometimes insist on pronouncing long vowels in the English words, disregarding sound-changes which have taken place in these words.[1] A similar smattering of knowledge causes many people to use quite irrelevant arguments in support of particular pronunciations. One northerner with a strong anti- pathy to the southern long vowel in *path* felt that he had clinched the matter when he pointed out that the vowel must be short since the word contained no *r*. He had realised that a following *r* has caused lengthening of the *a* in words like *arm* but he had ignored the fact that there are many other causes of lengthening of vowels.

When we are confronted with two alternatives, we sometimes find that, for different reasons, they both sound wrong. When this happens, a frequent cause of the trouble is that there is a conflict between grammar and logic. Are the pronouns *everybody* and *everyone* singular or plural? They are generally regarded as grammatically singular, and in short sentences there is little temptation to use them with plural verbs, but in longer sentences there is less certainty. When we say 'every- body' we are generally thinking of a number of people, and when a sentence beginning with 'everybody' goes on to include

[1] See John Sargeaunt, *The Pronunciation of English Words Derived from the Latin*, S.P.E. Tract No. 4 (1920).

other pronouns, there is a strong tendency to slip into the plural. No great harm is done if we use 'everybody' with a plural verb, but an awkward sentence results if we have a singular and a plural verb referring to the actions of the same persons in the same sentence. 'Everybody should do as they like' is less likely to distract the reader's attention from the subject-matter than 'Everybody has the right to do as they like'. One reason for the use of the plural pronouns *they* and *their* after *everybody* is that they can refer to both men and women, and we are thus confronted with the alternatives 'Everybody should do as they like', which may be thought ungrammatical, or 'Everybody should do as he or she likes', which will certainly be thought pedantic. Fortunately, a writer or speaker is hardly ever in a position where he has only two alternatives. It is generally possible to use a different construction, such as 'We can all do as we like'. Grammar and logic are not the only requirements to be satisfied; it is perfectly proper for a writer to reject a construction because he doesn't like the rhythm or because he can't imagine anyone using these words.

In everyday life people get into the way of using familiar phrases with little thought about the meaning. It is very natural that a man repairing a television set, after correcting one fault, should ask if there are others by saying 'Is it all right otherwise?' One salesman asked this question about a set which was working perfectly well. When asked what he meant by 'otherwise', he replied rather sulkily 'It's just an expression'. There may be similar difficulty in appreciating the inconsistencies implicit in one's own remarks. One customer in a shop found his annoyance swallowed up in delight when an assistant told him with some asperity 'As I've already told six customers this morning, we don't stock it because there's no demand for it'. There is also an inappropriate use of idiom. A soldier grows accustomed to being 'issued with' indispensable articles of equipment, but it seemed to be not quite the right idiom when one soldier reported that he had not been issued with a bastardy order.

English spelling is notoriously inconsistent and it is rather hard on those whose only wish is to be left alone that failure to master its intricacies is sometimes regarded as one of the clearest signs of an inadequate education. It was not always so. A Middle English scribe would think nothing of spelling the same word in two different ways in a single line, and the early editions of Shakespeare's plays contain a wide variety of different spellings of the same word. Demand for conformity to the sometimes arbitrary spelling conventions of present-day English comes from the pedagogue rather than the philologist, but such conformity has practical advantages, as anyone who has either compiled or used a glossary to an Old English or Old French text can testify; variety of spelling entails the use of frequent cross-references and uncertainty about the identification of words. A philologist who becomes familiar with the wide variety of spelling current in Early English is in danger of forgetting the habits of good spelling that he acquired in his youth, and the marking of examination papers can induce a similar uncertainty.

7

Our Changing Language

To the various causes of the rise of different varieties of a language we must add another: the lapse of time. Languages are constantly changing, and in course of time the changes are so numerous that a new variety of the language can be recognised as having come into existence. Varieties of this kind are most obvious to the student of literature, since he covers a much longer period of time than the student of the spoken word, but even within the lifetime of one person a careful observer can detect changes in vocabulary, pronunciation and syntax that are enough to bring into existence new varieties of language. Old-fashioned pronunciations and turns of phrase continue to be used side by side with the newer usages that are replacing them. The newer usages at first escape detection or are dismissed as mistakes, but in course of time it becomes clear that they are used by the majority of speakers. Pronouncing dictionaries and grammars of contemporary English lag behind actual usage, since they are generally written by older speakers who tend to describe the speech-habits of their own formative years.

The measure of success of a writer on changes taking place in the English language today is that within a few decades of its publication most of what he has written will seem pointless to the general reader, because the changes whose beginnings he saw have been completed. It often comes as a surprise to find how recent are some established words and phrases.

Students of the history of the English language often find that the best way to understand what a sound-change really is is to notice sound-changes that are taking place at the present time, when it is possible to hear the old pronunciation and the new side by side, together with innumerable intermediate pronunciations used by different speakers.

All living languages are constantly changing, but the rate of change varies. Spoken language changes more quickly than written because it is more alive; the recording of a language in writing gives it a semblance of permanence that is contrary to the nature of language. The spoken language is like a living person growing older continuously but so slowly that it is hard to point to any one changing feature. The written records of a language are like a family photograph album preserving a series of synchronic records.

In studying changes that are taking place at the present day, two things must be constantly remembered. The first is that changes in pronunciation do not as a rule take place quickly; we have to think in decades rather than years, and during that time we can notice a gradual increase in the number of speakers who adopt a new linguistic feature. The second thing to remember is that time is only one of the variables. In order to observe a linguistic change it is necessary to isolate the variables, such as regional and class dialect, to make sure that we are comparing like with like.

Prescriptive grammarians encourage us to regard all linguistic change as sinful, at least at the time when it is taking place. The student of the history of a language need not accept this view, but its existence can be useful to him. We are able to gather valuable information about the past history of English from the writings of seventeenth and eighteenth-century grammarians who deplored the changes they described, and angry letters written to the newspapers today can call our attention to changes that are taking place even if we do not share the wrath of the writers. Changes are taking place in vocabulary, pronunciation and syntax, with the result that certain usages seem old-fashioned to younger speakers, although they have no difficulty in understanding their meanings. Thus, *motor-car* and *wireless* are more old-fashioned than *car* or *radio*.

When we read a play or a novel written twenty or thirty years ago, we often feel that the dialogue is old-fashioned, though we may have difficulty in selecting specific examples in support of this view. Change in language is only one of the possible causes of this impression. There is always the possibility that fashions of play-writing have changed and that stage dialogue is today more realistic than it used to be.

Mass media of communication (newspapers, cinema, radio, television) and popular education encourage uniformity. Newspapers do not affect pronunciation but all four mass media affect syntax and vocabulary. Even if there is no deliberate attempt to 'correct' the dialect speech of schoolchildren, it is not usual for dialect to be the deliberate medium of instruction. It is necessary to say 'deliberate' because many schoolteachers themselves speak a regional dialect without realising it. The effect of the various standardising influences is to remove the extreme forms of dialect without necessarily increasing the number of speakers of standard English; the number of speakers of 'modified standard' is increased.

Standard English owes much to the public schools. Daniel Jones claims that his *Pronouncing Dictionary of English* records the pronunciation usually heard 'in the families of Southern English people who have been educated at the public schools'. The vocabulary of upper-class English is easier to acquire than its pronunciation, and class-indicators like *serviette* and *napkin*, *toilet* and *lavatory* soon cease to have any significance as features of class dialect.

Since the Second World War there has been an increase in the number of professional men who do not speak standard English and a reduction in the number of people who go out of their way to acquire it. There has probably been an increase in hostility to 'talking posh': the use of standard English as a result of conscious effort by speakers to whom it does not come naturally. Mr Charles Barber comments on the attitude towards standard English during the Second World War:

One of the first linguistic facts that many of us must have noticed when we passed through the ranks at the beginning of the last War was the speed and unanimity with which a barrack-room would react against anybody thought to be putting on linguistic airs ('talking posh' or 'talking la-di-da'); officers of course were different – they were expected to talk like that – though an officer with a particularly marked upper-class accent was always liable to be mimicked behind his back (especially if disliked for other reasons). This kind of hostility seems now to be appearing among the professional classes, among the new intelligentsia produced by the educational and social changes of the last few years.[1]

When we discuss a changing language we are concerned not only with changes of usage but with changes of acceptance. People have been splitting infinitives for centuries, but there are changes in the frequency with which infinitives are split and changes in the effect on the hearer.

The problems presented by a changing language are not confined to one part of the English-speaking community. Observers in America notice changes taking place in American English and comment on them with the same ferocity as that shown by British observers. One subject of hostile comment on both sides of the Atlantic is the influence of British and American English on each other. James Thurber complained of the pronunciation of a number of words: 'crippled or wingless words that escape, all distorted, the careless human lips of our jittery time'.[2] He has an interest in vocabulary and provides a useful detached observer's view when he says that the English begin almost every third sentence with the word 'actually', but his chief interest is in pronunciation. He records the pronunciations of *futile*, with the second syllable [il], [l] and [ail] respectively, saying that he prefers the first. He deplores the British pronunciation of *figure* as 'figga', thus siding with Robert Bridges in his hostility to the practice of reducing the vowel of lightly stressed syllables to [ə]. He accepts the British pronunciation of *schedule* as being, after all, 'a matter of schooling', but protests against the tendency of most Americans to say 'skedjuel' and of one of them to say 'skedjil'. He protests against the tendency of most Americans to pronounce words like *sparkling* and *evening* as three syllables.

The B.B.C. and their linguistic advisers are in a good position to study changes that are taking place in English pronunciation, because they receive many complaints about the pronunciation of announcers, and many of these complaints simply record the unwillingness of listeners to accept changes that are taking place. They have found that the younger the announcers the

---

[1] Barber, *Linguistic Change in Present-day English*, p. 26.

[2] James Thurber, 'Friends, Romans, Countrymen, Lend Me Your Ear Muffs', in *Lanterns and Lances* (Penguin Books, 1963).

more does their speech vary from the accepted norm.[1] This variation is the result of changes in language, the accepted norm being based on the speech of older speakers, who are reluctant to admit change.

Lloyd James, who advised the B.B.C. on linguistic matters, recorded sound-changes that were most frequently the subject of complaints in the 1930s.[2]

(1) The shortening of long open *o* before voiceless fricatives in words like *off* and *cough*.

(2) The raising of [æ] in the South to short open *e*, as in *hat* and *majesty*.

(3) The lowering of final [i] in words like *pity* and *city*.

(4) The retraction, lowering and lengthening of final [ə] to [ɑː], as in *pleasure* and *empire*.

(5) The monophthongisation of the triphthongs [aiə] and [auə] to [ɑː], as in *fire* and *power*.

(6) The retraction of the first element of the diphthongs [ai] and [au] to [ɑ], as in *my* and *found*.

We may add a few other changes in pronunciation that have become more marked since the time when Lloyd James wrote:

(7) The lowering of the first element of the diphthong [ei] to open *e*, as in *say* and *gate*.

(8) The centralising of the first element of the diphthong [ou] to a vowel approaching [ə] as in *go* and *coat*.

(9) The tendency, especially in the South, of the diphthong [ɔə] to become [ɔː] and of [uə] to become [ɔə] or [ɔː], as in *sore*, *four*, and *poor*, *moor*.

(10) The tendency of some speakers in the South to lengthen and raise the *o* before *l* in words like *solve* and *resolve*. The *l* sometimes disappears.

(11) The tendency to reduce the diphthong [ei] to [ə] in *railway*.

(12) The tendency to move the accent as near as possible to the first syllable of a word. This has affected disyllabic words, such as *ally* and *adult*, as well as longer words, such as *laboratory*.

[1] James, *The Broadcast Word*, p. 25.
[2] Ibid., pp. 161 f.

F

(13) An extension in the number of polysyllabic words in which a lightly-stressed [i] has disappeared. The loss took place in *medicine* some time ago, but it is now found, especially in upper-class speech, in such words as: *criminal, officer, promising, discipline, fascinating* and *hooliganism.*

Some pairs of words become homophones as the result of the falling together of sounds. The change of *wh* to *w* has led to the falling together of *which* and *witch, whither* and *wither, whine* and *wine.* Another group results from the loss of trilled *r* before a consonant: *father* and *farther, land* and *lord.* Robert Bridges[1] suggested that the verb *know* is doomed because various parts of it have homophones in *no, nose* and *new,* but these examples, all of them common words, show what a lot of homophony a language can stand provided that the homophones are not of a kind that can be substituted for one another. Bridges exaggerated the importance of homophones. It is true that the existence of homophones is one of many circumstances that *may* lead to the obsolescence of words; it does not follow that it *must* lead to obsolescence. Bridges was again being needlessly pessimistic when he said of the word *mourn*: 'If we persist in mispronouncing this word as *morn,* and make no distinction between *mourning* and *morning,* then that word will perish.'[2]

Air travel has greatly increased the number of Englishmen who have travelled abroad and the distances from home that they have reached. The chief linguistic result of this change is in the treatment of foreign proper names. Fifty years ago an Englishman would have felt self-conscious in using the foreign pronunciation of a place-name, even if he knew it; today there is a much better chance that he will have been to the place in question and that he will make some attempt to reproduce the foreign pronunciation, though sound-substitution is likely to take place if the name contains sounds that do not occur in English. In American English the attempt is less likely to be made, and personal names are especially liable to be pronounced as though they were English. No doubt pronunciation

---

[1] S.P.E. Tract No. 3, p. 22.
[2] Ibid., p. 47.

has been affected by the existence in America of large numbers of people with foreign names who are anxious to be treated as Americans.

The number of words in the English language is already very large and it is increasing every day. It is not uncommon to hear people speak approvingly of the richness of the English vocabulary, assuming that this is a virtue in a language, but it is not necessarily so. The number of words in a language is of interest only to lexicographers; what matters is the number of words that are generally used. It can be a nuisance to read a book by an author with a vocabulary much larger than our own, and it is a reflection of the resentment that we feel that *jargon* (technical vocabulary) has become a term of abuse. Within the large vocabulary of a language like English there is a smaller vocabulary of words that are familiar to most educated readers, though the number of words that they themselves use will be smaller still. It is this stock of generally understood words that constitutes the important vocabulary of a language, and the number of words that it contains is constantly fluctuating. As the inventors of Basic English realised, quite complicated ideas can be expressed after a fashion with a remarkably small vocabulary. We do not need to restrict our vocabulary so drastically as to use only the 850 words of Basic English, but a large vocabulary is an asset only if two conditions are satisfied: the words must be necessary and we must know how to control them. As knowledge extends, new words will be needed to describe the new ideas, but it is no gain to acquire another fifty synonyms to describe death or drunkenness or vague approval or disapproval. Words that express subtle shades of meaning are an asset if we are sensitive to such shades but a nuisance if we are not. A language, like a camera, can be too good for its users.

It is not as a rule possible to date the first use of a new word in a language. The date of the first recorded occurrence gives us a later limit, but many early records have been lost and a word may have been used in speech long before it was used in writing. To date the death of a word is even more difficult. Once it has been recorded in a book or dictionary it never completely dies. Long after it has become obsolete in general use, someone may see the word in a book, guess or look up its meaning, and use it if it happens to take his fancy. When we record the obsolescence of words we have to distinguish between active and passive survival. There are many words whose meaning we understand which we should never use ourselves because we think them too literary or old-fashioned. *Mannequin* is passing out of use, and has been replaced by *model*. Some words, such as *nice* and *get*, are avoided because excessive use makes fastidious writers unwilling to employ them; others, such as *blooming* and *shove*, pass out of use because their use as slang has given them a new meaning with ludicrous associations. Some words, such as *meed*, pass out of general use because the existence of homophones leads to ambiguity. Such words often survive as literary archaisms when they are no longer in colloquial use.

Words and meanings that have become obsolete in ordinary use are sometimes preserved in conventional phrases. People who would never speak of *moiling* in isolation both use and understand the phrase *toiling and moiling*, and the *hue* in *hue and cry* is quite a different word from the familiar *hue* meaning 'colour'. The old meaning of *meat* (food) is preserved in the proverb 'One man's meat is another man's poison' as well as in the compound word *sweetmeat*, and the proverb 'More haste less speed' preserves something of the meaning of O.E. *spēd* (success) beside the modern sense of 'rapid movement'.

The most common way of enriching the vocabulary of a language is by the introduction of loan-words from other languages. The interest of such words is not merely linguistic; we have borrowed things and ideas as well as the words used to describe them. An *anorak*, a jacket with a hood attached for use in cold climates, took its name from the Eskimos into Danish and was borrowed into English, becoming widely used in the 1950s. Another recent Scandinavian word is *ombudsman*, first borrowed in 1959 from Norwegian as the name of an official whose duty it is to investigate the complaints of citizens against other officials. In 1966 the British Government appointed an official with this function. His official title is Parliamentary Commissioner, but in popular speech he is generally called an ombudsman. One recent loan-word can be dated with unusual precision: the Russian word *sputnik* (artificial earth satellite), a word whose introduction followed quickly on the launching of the first space satellite in October 1957. *Karate* is from the Japanese word meaning 'empty-handed' and describes the art of fighting without weapons. The work of German-speaking psychologists has given us *Angst* (fear, anxiety) and *Schadenfreude* (pleasure in the troubles of others). From Afrikaans we have *apartheid*. *Moped* (motor-assisted pedal-cycle) did in fact originate in Sweden and quickly spread over Europe, though from the form alone it could have originated in England.

At any time it is possible to draw up a list of words which tend to be over-used for a time until the fashion for using them wanes. Sometimes, of course, these vogue-words are simply the reflection of vogue-ideas. The use of pipelines for the transport of oil is a feature of modern industry, so it is natural that there should be much talk of ideas being *in the pipeline* and that those who are concerned with *productivity* should be very interested in *throughput*. More often, however, vogue-words describe ideas that have always been important though their names change. A man will feel that he has adequately explained his failure to keep an appointment if he announces brightly that there has been a *breakdown of communication*. The prestige enjoyed by scientists extends to their vocabulary, and the technical language of sciences such as psychology and sociology, which are new in that they study old subjects in a new way, are particularly liable to be used as glamour-words. The introduction of a technical term, whose meaning is known neither to the speaker nor his hearers, sometimes serves the purpose of causing an impressionable audience to suspend judgement out of a feeling that they are out of their depth. It may be that poverty loses some of its sting when poor people are described as belonging to *lower income groups* or, to make it sound even more technical, *lower income brackets*. Vogue-words and phrases that arise from the use or misuse of technical terms of the social or natural sciences include *counter-productive, a traumatic experience, capital-intensive, labour-intensive, crash barrier*.

Vogue-words are not necessarily new words. It is quite common for a word to remain in the language for centuries, generally understood but little used, and then to enjoy a period of brief popularity. After this period when it is on everybody's lips, it may again sink into obscurity all the greater because careful speakers and writers have learnt to shun it as an over-used word. The use of vogue-words in political journalism is satirised in a cartoon in the *Daily Telegraph* (6 August 1970) which shows the Prime Minister and his colleagues considering a mountainous pile of pay claims. The Prime Minister is say-ing '. . . and finally, should we call it a norm, a pause, a squeeze, a freeze, restraint, or just a touch on the tiller?'

Human behaviour has no doubt followed the same broad, general lines as long as human beings have lived on the earth, but old-fashioned actions acquire an up-to-date look when they are given new names. An exchange of views is now liable to be called a *dialogue*, while the bitter rivalry that is found when no exchange is possible is called *infighting*. A man with qualities that impress his fellow-men is said to have *charisma*; a man with progressive views is said to be *forward-looking* and his views are *exciting* or *relevant*. The practice of mentioning the names of well-known people in order to gain reflected glory is known as *name-dropping*. A group of people within a larger group trying to inspire the rest with enthusiasm for action is described as a *ginger group*. Failure in understanding and communication between people of different ages is said to be due to the *genera-tion gap*.

New phrases have come into use to describe the conditions in which we live today. The meaning of some of them is self-evident; we have learnt the meaning of others so gradually that we do not often realise how new they are and how puzzling they might have been to our forefathers. They might manage to understand the meaning of *the Welfare State* or *science fiction*, but *the cold war* could have been puzzling. Improvements in arrangements for the care of the sick have made us familiar with the term *intensive care unit* in a hospital. The treatment of mental illness has given us *group therapy*, *aversion therapy* and *electro-convulsive therapy*, the last sometimes disguised by the euphemistic use of the initials *E.C.T.* The invention of new methods of mass communication has led to the use of the term *media* to describe them. The improvement of communication has led to the growth of devices for suppressing it, and from time to time we hear of a *D-notice* having been sent to the press. The D is for 'denial' and the term is used to describe a notice officially sent to newspapers asking them not to publish a particular piece of information. We have become familiar with the *P.R.O.*, the public relations officer who specialises in the control of information, and the term *de-brief* is used to describe the gathering of information from someone who has been sent on a mission. An *anchor man* is a man who ensures the smooth running of a television discussion, and a *link man* holds together the separate items in a programme. When we find someone whose attitude to life is similar to our own, we sigh with relief at finding somebody else who is *tuned in to the same wave-length*. No university is now complete without its *language laboratory*, where *tape-recording machines* are used in a room divided into cubicles. New inventions exert an influence on everyday life in many different ways. If we are suspected of having drunk too much before driving a car, we may be subjected to a *breathalyser test*; if we want to pay a bill we may use the *Giro*. Some of the new terms describe nuisances. We are all under the jurisdiction of courts of law, but some of us may find ourselves affected by the decisions of improperly constituted tribunals popularly known as *kangaroo courts*. We have learnt how to deal with advertisements and door-to-door salesmen, but we now have to cope with *inertia selling*, the practice of sending by post goods that have not been ordered in the hope that the recipient will pay for them to avoid the trouble of sending them back. Certain foods are unexpectedly cheap because they have been produced under the conditions of intensive production known as *factory farming*. The rise in the price of houses has given rise to the practice of *gazumping*: raising the price of a house after accepting a verbal offer but before signing a contract. The invention of the atomic bomb has led to the invention of new words and phrases and to a wider currency for others. We thus have *chain-reaction*, and words like *device* and *deterrent* acquire new sinister associations because they are so often used together with the word *nuclear*. Space travel has provided *cosmonaut*, *space-suit* and *retro-rocket*, and the practice of counting backwards which is adopted in the launching of a rocket has given the verb *to count down* and the noun *count-down*. *Blast-off*, which would once have been regarded as an intimation that one's presence was unwelcome, is now a noun describing the launching of a rocket.

The Second World War, like the First, brought into use many new words, some of which have survived war-time conditions. Many of these were familiar words used in new senses. *Basic* came to be used as a noun to describe the amount of petrol to which every motorist was entitled, and *pool petrol* was unbranded petrol. *Siren* meant only an air-raid siren. *Radar* was in origin an American expression, made up from initials (*radio detection and ranging*), but it is now firmly established in British English.

A useful word of recent introduction is *hindsight* (wisdom after the event), formed, no doubt, on the model of *foresight*. Another is *gimmick* (a device to attract publicity), borrowed from American English. The word satisfies a need because, with the development of advertising and public relations as professions, such devices have become increasingly common, and that not merely in the world of commerce. Another useful word is *teenager*, and we have borrowed a number of phrases like *in the red* from American English.

New names are needed for the products of modern techno-logical discovery, such as *nylon* and *penicillin*. Others arise from new scientific discoveries or concepts, such as *cybernetics*, *servo-mechanism*, *entropy* and *laser*. Some have come into ex-istence because of war. No doubt in the early years of the present century *fire-watcher*, if used at all, would describe a man fond of warming his feet at the fire and would have some of the derogatory associations of *clock-watcher*, a man who is anxious not to work too hard. Others are the reflection of social prob-lems or social change: *hippy*, *psychedelic*. Some words and phrases are widely used because they describe contemporary political conditions. The tendency of the nations of today to ally them-selves with either the United States or the Soviet Union has led to the use of the term *the Third World* to describe the un-aligned powers; the phrase is now often used as a synonym for what are sometimes described as the *underdeveloped* countries. When immigrants from these countries find themselves, from choice or necessity, living in separate areas, the word *ghettos* is used to describe those areas, with a loss of the old sense of the word to describe the Jewish quarters of towns. Politicians who pursue militant and conciliatory policies are known as *hawks* and *doves* respectively. The growing importance of radio and television and the rise of newspapers with enormous circulations have led

us to talk of the *mass media*. A sudden increase in numbers is
known as *escalation*, and an increase slightly larger than expected is an *explosion*. Vogue-words that do not describe modern
developments include *exciting*, *creative*, *prestigious*, *rat-race*,
consortium, *confrontation*, *grass roots*, *the silent majority*, *to pin-
point*, *updated*. What used to be called a committee is now *a
working party*. *Built-in* was originally used of physical objects,
such as wardrobes, but it has come to mean 'inherent'. A brand
of cigarettes has been described as having 'built-in consumer
appeal'. *Basically* is now a vogue-word, as may be seen not only
by the frequency with which it is used but by the frequency
with which it is used unreasonably. The following statement,
made by the Entertainments Manager of a seaside resort,
mixes the dignified and the slangy: 'After the strikes and short-
time working of the winter people are basically broke' (*Daily
Telegraph*, 29 July 1969).

In the field of music what used to be called a gramophone is
now usually called a *record-player*; what used to be called a
gramophone record is now called a *disc* or an *L.P.* Presumably
the latter term will pass out of use when it comes to be taken
for granted that all records in general use are long-playing.
One of the most fashionable professions of the present day is
that of introducing records on the radio, and those who follow
this profession are known as *disc jockeys* or *d.j.'s*.

There has been a very great increase in the use of *hopefully*
in sentences where it is not certain who is doing the hoping.
Three instances occurred in the City pages of a single issue of a
newspaper (*Daily Telegraph*, 1 August 1970):

But all five theatres are subject to current negotiations, which
hopefully will lead to greater profitability.

The 'Cambridge' launch and promotion apart, Carreras
was clobbered on three counts in the second half, all of
which, hopefully, are non-recurring.

Hopefully, the report will go out to shareholders ... 'not
later than August 27'.

Just as there are vogue-words, so there are phrases which
enjoy great popularity for a brief period. Most of these tend

to be slang or colloquialisms. For a time people were urging one another *to do their own thing* or to *keep their cool*, expressing enthusiastic agreement with *You can say that again* or acceding to a request with the words *Be my guest*. At a slightly more formal level we have *the corridors of power* to describe influential groups of administrators, and *That is what — is all about*, with a strong stress on the last word. When a phrase is first used it often expresses a shade of meaning which is lost when the phrase becomes fashionable. *I wouldn't know* originally meant more than *I don't know*. It meant 'I don't know, and only a fool would expect me to', but the phrase gradually lost this discourteous shade of meaning. Now that it means much the same as *I don't know* and has no longer the recommendation of novelty, there is no particular reason why it should continue to exist.

Many people who conform to tradition in most linguistic matters feel free to experiment in the choice of proper names. The names of houses may be acquired by new owners long after their origin has been forgotten. Deliberately fanciful names are perhaps less common than they used to be. Place-names are often used as house-names, to the confusion of letter-sorters. One house-name that at first seems to be of this kind is *Thursley*, but the existence of neighbouring houses called *Wensley* and *Frysley* leads one to suspect a more fanciful origin. Neighbours are apprehensive lest one of the houses near should take on the name *Sattersleigh*. In choosing names for children most people are fortunately content to be conventional; Max Beerbohm gives a graphic account of the sufferings at a prepatory school of a boy whose parents were not so content and gave him the name Ladbroke. The transitory nature of fame is illustrated by the practice of naming children after people prominent in the news. It is not only film stars whose names are forgotten by the time that the children named after them have grown up. In one village a Redvers and a Garnet were well known long after Sir Redvers Buller and Sir Garnet Wolseley were forgotten by most of the inhabitants. The same fate could hardly be expected to overtake a man whose forename was Gladstone, but its origin was concealed by the pet-forms *Gladdy* and *Stoney*.

Semantic change is a slow and gradual process and instances of it that we can see in operation today are for the most part portions of processes that began a long time ago. The changes that are taking place today are similar to those that took place in the past, but there is one kind of semantic change that is especially common today: extension of meaning resulting from the misuse of technical terms. This is a result of the great advances that have been made in scientific and technical discovery. Each branch of knowledge has developed its own technical vocabulary, the exact meaning of which is known only to specialists. The general public hears the technical terms and has an excessive trust in their wonder-working properties. Tony Weller was convinced that Mr Pickwick would not have lost the case of *Bardell* v. *Pickwick* if only he had had an alibi, and many others after him have thought that an *alibi* was any sort of evidence of innocence. Its technical sense as a legal term is closely linked with its etymology (Latin *alibi*, 'elsewhere'). It is a plea that the accused was somewhere else when the crime was committed, and therefore cannot be guilty of committing it. Since the invention of the atom bomb, *atomic*, once coupled with words like *weight* or *theory*, has acquired strong emotional associations. It is generally assumed to refer to nuclear fission rather than to atoms in general, and association with the idea of tremendous power has made it a glamour word. A laundry is described by its owners as 'atomic' and one is left wondering whether it blows the clothes to bits or whether a scholarly laundry proprietor is thinking of the etymology of the word (Greek 'something which cannot be divided') and is promising that clothes entrusted to him will not be torn.

Love of technical terms does not always result in misunderstanding; sometimes the only result is pretentiousness. The prefix *non-* has a rather learned sound, and consequently many people prefer to say that certain things are non-existent rather than that there aren't any. One man who couldn't read gave his disability quite a learned sound when he was handed a telegram: 'Nay, I'm a non-scholar.'

The meaning of a word can vary very much from one environment to another. Those who are proud to call themselves Liberals may be rather puzzled by the question attributed to a little girl brought up in a staunch Conservative family: 'Mother, are Liberals born bad or do they become so?' The mother's reply was uncompromising: 'They are born bad and become worse.'

Many new compound words have come into use to describe new inventions or social trends. A *bubble-car* is a motor-car with a plastic roof that looks like a large bubble, and a *frogman* is a diver using equipment that makes him look like a frog. Books bound in paper covers are no new invention, but they have in recent years become so much more common that we have felt the need of the word *paperback* to describe them. A number of American compound words have been borrowed into British English because they serve a useful purpose. Such words are *baby-sitter, gate-crasher, stockpile* and *bulldozer*. There is also the useful verb *to debunk*, meaning 'to expose pretentious claims', and the less common verb, used satirically, *to rebunk* meaning 'to re-establish a reputation that has been destroyed by debunking'.

One type of compound noun that has become especially common recently is that made up of a verb followed by an adverb. Some of these nouns are still regarded as compound words needing hyphens; others have come to be accepted as single words. A *showdown* is a metaphor from the game of poker, where it describes the laying down of cards on the table with their faces up; figuratively it mean a final test or disclosure of achievements or possibilities. Other examples are: *hand-out* (official statement intended primarily for the press), *slow-down* (diminution of speed), *run-down* (reduction in numbers, especially of armed forces by demobilisation), *build-up* (favourable publicity for a person or product). The prolixity of the definitions is a measure of the usefulness of the words, but this type of compound has become too fashionable. How does a *walk-out* differ from a strike? It may sometimes be used of a strike without union recognition, though for this term *wildcat strike* is now widely used. Some of the compounds do not seem very happy. For example, we hear much of *teach-ins*, but the essential characteristic of a *teach-in* is the emphasis on discussion rather than on teaching.

New words are often formed, in spite of protests, by the addition of prefixes and suffixes to familiar words. Such coinages are made to meet temporary needs, such as those of war, and pass out of use with the return of more normal conditions.

Examples are *decontaminate* (remove the effects of contamination), *derestrict* (remove restrictions from), *derequisition* (return a requisitioned property to its owner), *inter-allied* (between allies), *evacuee* (child removed from a town to a safer country district). Abstract nouns of great length are formed in this way by the addition of suffixes to words which already contain suffixes. Such words tend to be used pejoratively, as *revisionist, sensationalism*.

Sometimes one prefix is mistaken for another, and the mistake can affect the meaning of the word in which it occurs. *Protagonist* is from a Greek word meaning the actor who takes the chief part in a play, and hence it comes to mean the chief personage in any affair. But the Greek prefix *protos* (first) has been confused with the Latin prefix *pro-* (on behalf of), and the word is now often used in the sense of 'advocate, champion'. The addition of suffixes is a common and legitimate way of modifying the meanings of words. No one would claim that *sense* has the same meaning as *sensibility* or *sentiment* the same as *sentimentality*. Unfortunately the difference in meaning conferred by a suffix is often so subtle that it can easily be lost, and there is a tendency to add suffixes needlessly. People often say *transportation* when they mean *transport*, and parsons sometimes describe their visiting as *visitation*. Partly as a result of American influence, verbs in *-ise* are becoming more common and the result is to make simple actions seem needlessly complicated. *Verbalise* is used instead of *speak* and a man who goes into hospital is said to undergo *hospitalisation*. There is no reason to outlaw any kind of word-formation, but some of the verbs in *-ise* and the abstract nouns in *-isation* seem needlessly long and pedantic. A weather report was described as being of special interest to 'those who are motorised at this point in time'. There are many legitimate ways of describing a motorist, but this is surely not one of them. The Open University is one of the most interesting educational experiments of the present century, and it has begun to develop its own language. One student writes that the possibility of being lost in the Open University computer is a real one:

The student's great fear is that, to use Orwell's word, he will be rendered Unperson. The Open has its own terms for this. Students misplaced by the computer are said to be 'unstructured' or 'randomised'.

Daily Telegraph, 11 December 1971

American influence can be used to explain the growing fondness for adverbs ending in *-wise*. The ending is found in many adverbs, such as *clockwise*, *anticlockwise* and *likewise*, but until recently it was not a living suffix that could be used to make new adverbs. All this is now changed and we get such words as *fashionwise*.

Length can be a real drawback to the use of a word which has been formed on perfectly defensible lines. *Meteorological* is a clumsy word to describe a perfectly familiar thing, and it is not surprising that radio announcers have got into the way of speaking familiarly of the *Met. Office*. In most polysyllabic words the first syllable is the most significant, and the usual type of shortening is therefore that which involves the loss of the ending of a word, as in *pub*, but in *bus* it is the beginning that has disappeared. The inter-communication system of an aeroplane was a natural candidate for shortening and so we get *intercom*. *Poliomyelitis* becomes *polio*. *Prefab*, like *intercom*, involves the shortening of the first word of a phrase and the loss of the second.

A number of blend-words have become well established in the language. *Napalm* is made up from *naphthalene* and *palm*, *motel* from *motor* and *hotel*, *smog* from *smoke* and *fog*, *subtopia* from *suburb* and *Utopia*.

Back-formations are liable to occur at any time. So long as we remain conscious of their origin, they are generally confined to slang and colloquial speech. Examples are *to enthuse* from *enthusiastic*, *to liaise* from *liaison* and *to reminisce* from *reminiscence*. Some back-formations are little more than nonce-words, created as a joke; one such word is *to frivol* (to behave frivolously).

Words made from initials are known as *acronyms* and they are playing an increasing part in our lives. Even if the initials do not form a pronounceable word, they may pass into general use if they stand for scientific terms too long to be acceptable. Thus, *T.N.T.* and *P.V.C.* are used by large numbers of people only a few of whom know that they stand for *trinitrotoluene* and *polyvinyl chloride*. If the initials can be pronounced as a word, they have a better chance of acceptance, and so we have *radar* [reidɑː] and *Rada* [rɑːdə], with an arbitrary but useful distinction in pronunciation, standing respectively for 'radio direction and ranging' and 'Royal Academy of Dramatic Art'. These two words illustrate two of the rules of the game of word-creation from initials; unimportant words like *of* and *the* can be ignored, and more than one letter can be taken from a phrase if doing so helps to produce a word easy to pronounce: a good example is *laser* – 'light amplification by stimulated emission of radiation'. Words that have been created in this way, without ever becoming household words, include *Rospa* (Royal Society for the Prevention of Accidents) and *Bolsa* (Bank of London and South America). Others, more familiar, are *Naafi* [næfi] (Navy, Army and Air Force Institute) and *Unesco* [juːneskou] (United Nations Educational, Scientific and Cultural Organisation). Not all groups of initials that can be made into words are treated in this way. We perhaps feel that it would be disrespectful to call a V.I.P. (Very Important Person) a *vip*, and the Royal Air Force is treated in both ways: the R.A.F. [ði ɑːreiˈef] is normal standard English while *the Raf* [ðə ˈræf] is slang or colloquial.

When nouns describing occupations have distinctive forms to describe women, these are tending to disappear. Three categories can be distinguished. There are nouns like *doctor* and *writer* which have no distinctive forms for the feminine; there are pairs like *actor* and *actress*, *waiter* and *waitress*, where the feminine forms are so frequent that the absence of the feminine suffix will give rise to the assumption that the person referred to is a man; and there are words like *editor* and *chairman* which have feminine forms (*editress*, *chairwoman*) which can be used though they are unusual. It is usually possible to indicate the sex by the addition of another word, as for example *woman doctor*. When it is necessary to address a woman chairman formally, two approaches are possible: the old-fashioned and unrealistic *Mr Chairman* and the apparently self-contradictory *Madam Chairman*. Similarly, when a woman becomes the civic head of a city, she is called the Lord Mayor, not the Lady Mayoress, a title reserved for the wife of the Lord Mayor or for some other woman appointed to perform her social duties.

The use of one part of speech for another is common in modern English because there are very few formal criteria which distinguish one part of speech from another. *Love* may be derived from the Old English verb *lufian* or the noun *lufu*; the two forms have fallen together by the normal operation of phonetic change. It then becomes an easy matter to extend the process of conversion to other words which did not have a double origin. Interchange between nouns and verbs is particularly common: *to steam-roller* (what one does to opposition), *to feature*, *to accession* (in a library), *to audition*. In spite of the frequency of this functional shift, some examples of the use of nouns as verbs arouse violent opposition; the chief object of attack is the verb *to contact*. This verb is briefer than *to get in touch with* and it is useful to have a word that does not specify whether the contact shall be by speech, letter or telephone. A university department, sending out information about its open days for sixth-formers, asked those who would like notice of the next one to 'please card Dr B. S. Cox'. The secretary of one school reported that, as she was unable to support the cardisation of Dr Cox, she papered and enveloped him instead (*Daily Telegraph* 18 January 1968). *To ad-lib* is from an abbreviated Latin adverbial phrase. The use of verbs as nouns is less common, but we have *a must* (something indispensable). Nouns are used attributively to perform the function of adjectives, as in *utility furniture*, but they are not adjectives, as may be seen by such tests as the absence of comparison, or of predicative use or use with adverbs. There are examples of the converse process of the use of an adjective as a noun. Here the adjective is often used as a shortened form of a phrase consisting of adjective and noun, and the noun is understood, as in *the briny* (the sea), *the rich* (rich people). The use of one part of speech for another is thus well established in English, though it is less common today than it was in Elizabethan times.

Comparison of adjectives with *more* and *most* is gaining on the use of *-er* and *-est*, especially if the adjectives are at all long or unusual.

In nouns the *s*-genitive is gaining on the *of*-genitive. Until recently the *s*-genitive was generally used only with persons. Its growing use is a reversal of the normal English trend from inflectional endings to prepositions. A similar distinction between persons and things is breaking down in the use of *whose* and *which*. Until recently *whose* was normally used only of persons, but now it is increasingly used instead of *of which* in relation to things.

There is a tendency to omit the definite article before some words where it was once usual, such as *university* and *Government*. The phrase *going to university* has been described as substandard, but the parallel of *going to school* shows that there is nothing contrary to English idiom in the omission of the definite article in such a phrase. Logically it is the inclusion of the definite article, not its omission, that needs defence, since as a rule it is not one particular university that is referred to; the meaning could properly be expressed by saying *going to a university*. The omission of the definite article before *Government* is something of a fashionable affectation and it is sometimes used by members of the Government themselves.

In recent years there has been a great increase in the number of verb-phrases consisting of a verb and an adverb. The verbs most often used in this way are *get, put* and *try*. Sometimes the adverb seems unnecessary, as in *start up* (a car engine). The verb-phrase is often followed by a preposition, and here both adverb and preposition sometimes seem unnecessary, as in *meet up with*. Whatever objections there may be to the greeting *Pleased to meet you*, they are not removed if one says *Glad to meet up with you socially*. *Get* is used increasingly to form a passive, as in *he got hurt*.

Transitive verbs are always liable to be used intransitively; the process was especially frequent in Elizabethan English. Today we can see it taking place with certain verbs. Until recently *identify* was normally used as a transitive verb; its direct object was often a reflexive pronoun, such as 'oneself'. There is an increasing tendency, especially in literary and dramatic criticism, to omit the pronoun, and a critic will complain that he is not able to identify with any of the characters in a play or novel under discussion.

One idiom that flourishes in colloquial speech today is the use of *do a* followed by a proper name with the meaning 'to behave like that person'. This kind of idiom flourishes best among fairly homogeneous groups, who are likely to understand the allusions. John Osborne uses it in *Look Back in Anger* (1956), where, in a stage direction, two men are described as doing a Flanagan and Allen (Act III, scene i). The number of people able to understand the allusion would at one time have been very large but it is decreasing every day.

A colloquial construction that has become common in recent years is an import from America, though it may ultimately be of German origin. This consists of inverting the usual position of subject and verb in order to gain emphasis. The inversion gives a sentence the form of a question, but the intonation makes clear the difference between *Was I glad to hear your voice?* and *Was I glad to hear your voice!* Another construction that was widely current for some years after the Second World War is now less often heard. This is a way of indicating that a statement that one has oneself made is open to argument, and it consists of a short question introduced by *Or*. The simplest form of the question could be *Or is it?* but the exact form is dictated by the form of the statement in which the speaker wishes to cast doubt. For example, one might say *He is one of the greatest statesmen that have ever lived. Or is he?* A rather different use of a short question after a statement is found especially in lower-class speech and is perhaps used by men more often than women. Here the questioner, who is often himself replying to a question which he resents, appeals to his hearer for confirmation of a statement, even though it is one which the hearer is not in a position either to confirm or to contradict. It has a partial parallel in the use of French *N'est-ce-pas?* When used in English it tends to sound truculent, as in: *Where did you get that tobacco? I got it from the shop round the corner, didn't I? Want* is often used for *ought*, as in *You want to be careful*.

There are many different kinds of adverb – adverbs of place, of time, and so on – and we might add to the number of categories by speaking of adverbs of diffidence such as *really* in the sentence *I really think you ought to go home*. Two phrases are often used in this way, especially in conversation, in defiance of old-fashioned ideas of sentence-construction. These are *sort of* and *kind of*. They are equivalent to parenthetic clauses like *so to speak* and *as it were*. The excessive use of *sort of* can become a mannerism and is not confined to substandard speakers. A professor, who was trying not to be dogmatic, used the phrase more than a dozen times in the course of a short speech.

Two objections are sometimes made to the study of present-day English of the kind that has been attempted in this book. One is that the result is a mass of detail in which it is difficult to establish general trends. The reply to this objection is surely that generalisations based upon the observation of a large number of details have more value than those which have no such basis. Another objection is that the study of a language should be pursued more scientifically, with field-workers interviewing carefully selected samples of the population. All this will no doubt come in time. What is needed at present is the bringing together of a number of impressions in order to discover what are the fields that are most likely to repay a closer and more scientific investigation. The advantages of the study of varieties of English greatly outweigh the disadvantages. Quite apart from the contribution to our knowledge of the language that can be made by such a study, the observer, by the mere act of observing, develops his own sensitivity to shades of meaning, of pronunciation and of syntactic usage. The foreigner learning English gains a more effective knowledge of the language and the native speaker of English learns to make a fuller and better use of the medium which chance has placed within his reach.

Further Reading

1. Introduction

Randolph Quirk, *The Use of English* (Longmans, 1962; enlarged 2nd ed., 1968) is an excellent survey of many different aspects of English, with a number of exercises and topics for discussion at the end of each chapter. It has supplementary chapters by A. C. Gimson and Jeremy Warburg. Henry Bradley, 'On the Relations between Spoken and Written Language with Special Reference to English', *Proceedings of the British Academy* (1913) pp. 211–32, is still an important study. G. L. Brook, 'Varieties of English', *Bulletin of the John Rylands Library*, LI (1968–9) 271–91, deals briefly with the varieties of English other than dialects. Simeon Potter, *Our Language* (Penguin Books, 1950) is a lucid study of many aspects of English, both historical and contemporary. Ifor Evans, *The Use of English* (MacGibbon & Kee, 1949; 2nd ed., 1966) is a readable account of the use of English, especially in literature. Ernst Leisi, *Das Heutige Englisch* (Heidelberg: Carl Winter, 1955) includes chapters on many aspects of contemporary English, including vocabulary, slang, dialect and American English, with useful suggestions for further reading. P. D. Strevens's article 'Varieties of English' was first published in *English Studies*, XLV (1964), and has been reprinted in his book *Papers in Language and Language Teaching* (O.U.P., 1965).

2. Dialects

G. L. Brook, *English Dialects* (André Deutsch, 1963; 2nd ed., 1965) deals with both regional and class dialects. David Abercrombie, *Studies in Phonetics and Linguistics* (O.U.P., 1965) includes articles on 'Conversation and Spoken Prose' and 'R.P. and Local Accent'. J. Y. T. Greig, *Breaking Priscian's Head* (Kegan Paul, n.d., a volume in the 'To-day and To-morrow' series published in the 1920s) is a vigorous attack on some conventional views about the importance of standard English.

William Matthews, *Cockney Past and Present* (Routledge, 1938) places Cockney English in its historical setting. There is a discussion of English class dialects in A. S. C. Ross's article 'U and Non-U: An Essay in Sociological Linguistics', included in *Noblesse Oblige*, ed. Nancy Mitford (Hamish Hamilton, 1956). The standard work on the language of children is Iona and Peter Opie, *The Lore and Language of Schoolchildren* (O.U.P., 1959).

3. Idiolects

A. C. Gimson, *An Introduction to the Pronunciation of English* (Edward Arnold, 1962; 2nd ed., 1970) is an introduction to the pronunciation of contemporary English within the framework of general phonetics. Ida C. Ward, *The Phonetics of English* (Cambridge: Heffer, 1929; 4th ed., 1945) includes much information about variant pronunciations as well as chapters on 'Broadcasting and Spoken English' and 'Spelling Pronunciations'. Logan Pearsall Smith's 'English Idioms', originally published as an S.P.E. Tract in 1922, was reprinted in an expanded form in his *Words and Idioms* (Constable, 1925). W. E. Collinson, *Contemporary English: A Personal Speech Record* (Leipzig: Teubner, 1927) was intended primarily for foreign students of English, but it contains much useful material, recorded by a trained linguist, about the English language in the early years of the twentieth century.

4. Registers

Sir Ernest Gowers, *Plain Words* (H.M.S.O., 1948) and *A.B.C. of Plain Words* (H.M.S.O., 1951) were written at the invitation of the Treasury to improve the English used by Government officials. They are useful for the information that they provide about one register of English, but they have been found useful for their sensible comments on English usage by a body of readers much larger than that for which they were originally intended. The two books were combined as *The Complete Plain Words* in 1954 and this book was reissued by Penguin Books in 1962. A. Lloyd James, *The Broadcast Word* (Kegan Paul, 1935) is a collection of lectures and essays by a Professor of Phonetics who was Honorary Secretary of the B.B.C. Advisory

Committee on Spoken English. Heinrich Straumann, *Newspaper Headlines: A Study in Linguistic Method* (Allen & Unwin, 1935) is a systematic account of one aspect of the English of newspapers. Geoffrey N. Leech, *English in Advertising* (Longmans, 1966) is a useful objective study of an important variety of English, with numerous examples. I. A. Richards, *Basic English and Its Uses* (Kegan Paul, 1943) is a useful account of Basic English by one of its inventors. T. H. Savory, *The Language of Science* (André Deutsch, 1953) is an excellent study, written by a biologist, of the contribution of science to the English vocabulary. The extent to which games develop special vocabularies is illustrated by W. J. Lewis, *The Language of Cricket* (O.U.P., 1934), which includes more than a thousand main entries, with illustrative quotations.

5. Slang

The best and fullest account of slang, considered historically, is Eric Partridge, *Slang To-day and Yesterday*, 2nd ed. (Routledge, 1935). Several of the essays in the same author's *Words, Words, Words!* (Methuen, 1933) and *Here, There and Everywhere* (Hamish Hamilton, 1950) deal with various aspects of slang. Wilfred Granville, *A Dictionary of Theatrical Terms* (André Deutsch, 1952) includes much theatrical slang as well as technical terms.

6. Usage

Attitudes to English Usage, by W. H. Mittins and others (O.U.P., 1970) records the results of an inquiry to find the attitude of 500 people, mainly teachers and students, towards 55 disputed points of English usage. Sir Arthur Quiller-Couch, *On the Art of Writing* (C.U.P., 1916) is a series of lectures dealing with the writing of both verse and prose. H. W. Fowler, *A Dictionary of Modern English Usage* (O.U.P., 1926) gives forthright and sensible advice on English usage. It is a book for browsing in as well as for reference. A second edition, revised by Sir Ernest Gowers, was published in 1965. Eric Partridge, *Usage and Abusage: A Guide to Good English* (Hamish Hamilton, 1947; 5th ed., 1957; first published in the U.S.A. 1942) was intended to complement and supplement Fowler. Robert Graves and

Alan Hodge, *The Reader over Your Shoulder* (Cape, 1943) has
a long introduction dealing with the writing of English prose,
followed by a detailed examination of a number of prose ex-
tracts. This is a book to be used critically. The rewritten passages are a warning against a hypercritical approach to writing;
in losing their 'faults' the chosen passages have lost their
individuality of style. An abridged edition is now available.
Essays on Language and Usage, ed. Leonard F. Dean and Kenneth
G. Wilson (New York: O.U.P., 1959) reprints a number of
essays on the history, structure and use of English, thirteen of
them dealing with usage in general and with several detailed
questions.

7. Our Changing Language

Charles Barber, *Linguistic Change in Present-Day English* (Edinburgh: Oliver & Boyd, 1964), Brian Foster, *The Changing
English Language* (Macmillan, 1968), and Simeon Potter,
Changing English (André Deutsch, 1969) all examine changes
that are taking place in the English language today. The
effects of the Second World War on the English language
have been recorded by R. W. Zandvoort and his assistants in
Wartime English (Groningen: Wolters, 1957). This survey does
not as a rule include slang, technical terms or exclusively
American forms. Barbara M. H. Strang, *A History of English*
(Methuen, 1970) is a history working backwards from the
present day. It includes much useful information about
changes that have taken place within living memory.

Index

Words, but not phrases, quoted as examples are included in italics. No references are given to the authors of books recommended for further reading on pages 184–7.